TEXTILE & LAUNDRY IN HOTEL INDUSTRY

DR. D.K. Aggarwal
PRINCIPAL
INSTITUTE OF HOTEL MANAGEMENT &
CATERING TECHNOLOGY
BHOPAL (M.P.)

AMAN PUBLICATIONS
NEW DELHI (INDIA)

Published by
Rajiv Jain for Aman Publications
LG-4A, Ganpati Bhawan,
4675-B/21, Ansari Road,
Darya Ganj, Delhi - 110002
PH: 23255012, 23282127
E-mail: sshjbs@yahoo.com

First Edition 2006
ISBN-81-8204-024-8 (HB)

SOLE DISTRIBUTOR
JINDAL BOOK SERVICES
LG-4A, Ganpati Bhawan,
4675-B/21, Ansari Road,
Darya Ganj, Delhi - 110002

Laser Typesetting by:
S.M. Graphics, Delhi,

Printed by:
NCT Printers & Publishers , Delhi, India

PREFACE

Laundering is one of the most important part of housekeeping operations. Almost every large hotel has in-house laundry facility. In the 'good old days' laundry was done with soaps, scrub boards, wash tubs and lots of elbow grease. Today's advanced washing machines, hi-tech detergents and laundry additives make wash days easier and more successful, especially with the array of fabrics used in contemporary clothing. The laundry basics, however, haven't changed and are more important than ever.

This book is an indispensable guide to caring for all cloth in a hotel: from kitchen rags to bedding, hand-washables, and table clothes to window curtains. It offers detailed guidance on selecting and maintaining hotel clothing and fabrics, installing carpets, curtains and rugs, arraning table linens, removing stains, and making environmentally informed choices. It also provides readers with a seamless combination of reliable information, time-saving guidelines, and fascinating narratives on textile and laundry in the hotel industry.

CONTENTS

Contents

1

Hotel Laundry Operations

Hotel laundry is divided into two operations done by two separate groups of workers. Sorting, washing and drying towels is completed by one group of two workers. Drying (except for towels) and folding is completed by another group of six workers.

Sorting and Washing

In hotel, housekeepers use a laundry chute to get the dirty linen from the upstairs down to the laundry area. The sorting and washing operation involves the following:

— sorting laundry

— loading bins which weigh 60 pounds of dry laundry, and 120 pounds when wet

— transporting (pushing/pulling) bins to washer

— loading washer

— unloading washer

— transporting (pushing/pulling) bins to dryer (towels only)

— loading dryer with towels

— unloading towels from the dryer

Figure 1. Sorting laundry

In one eight-hour shift, 20 bins of laundry are processed by two workers (Figure 1.). The dry laundry is handled four times (60 lbs x 4 handlings x 20 bins = 4,800 lbs); the wet laundry is handled twice (120 lbs x 2 handlings x 20 bins = 4,800 lbs). The workload is distributed evenly, so each worker handles approximately 4,800 lbs or 2,200 kg of laundry every day.

The handling of the laundry requires the use of considerable force:

— pulling laundry from the pile under the chute (Figure 2, 3)

Figure 2.

Figure 3.

Pulling laundry pulling laundry from the pile under the chute

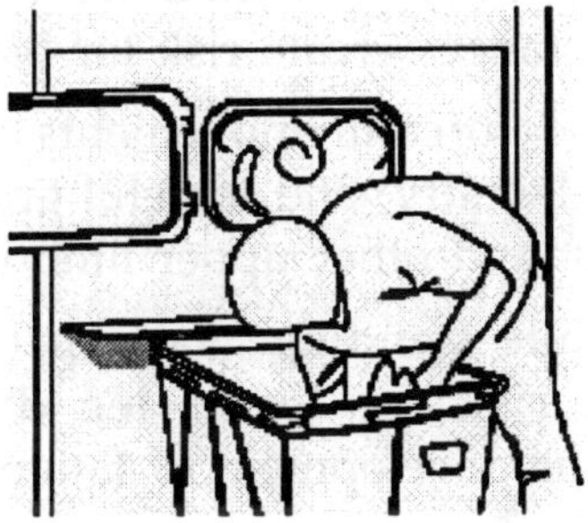

Figure 4. Loading the washer

— loading laundry into the washer (Figure 4)

— pulling wet laundry from the washer (Figure 5)

These movements are particularly stressful on the hands, wrists and shoulders.

Handling the laundry requires whole body motions beyond acceptable ranges. Reaching above the shoulder, bending to the floor (Figure 5) and twisting are examples. In addition, the job is carried out while standing on a concrete floor which adds stress to the feet and legs as well as to the rest of the body. Carrying out the sorting and washing tasks can be hazardous to the workers.

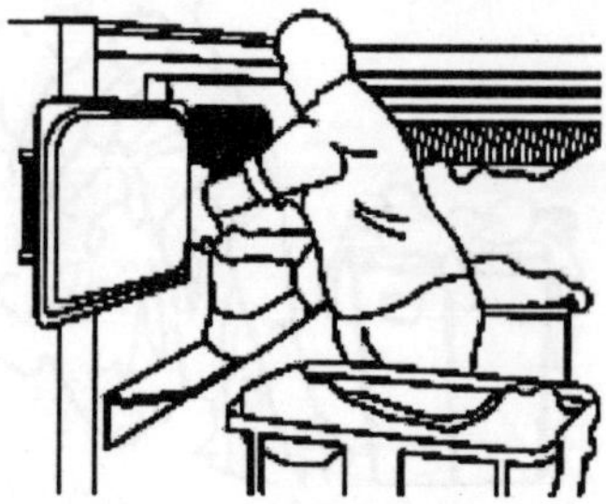

Figure 5. Pulling wet laundry from the washer

There are three major risk factors:

— The heavy work load (handling over 2 tonnes of laundry per shift) combined with bodily motions beyond safe ranges create risk for back injuries.

— Frequent and forceful movements (while pulling/pushing the laundry) and forceful grips create a high risk for wrist and other upper limb injuries.

— Working while standing/walking on a hard floor creates the risk for lower leg discomfort, and accelerates the development of fatigue.

These factors have a compounding effect. In other words, each of them increases the effect of the others.

Drying and Folding

There are three workstations at which five different tasks are performed:

— feeding the rolling dryer with small pieces of laundry (Figure 6)

— feeding the rolling dryer with large pieces of laundry (Figure 7)

— retrieving small pieces of laundry from the rolling dryer (Figure 8)

— retrieving large pieces of laundry from the rolling dryer (Figure 9)

— folding towels (Figure 10)

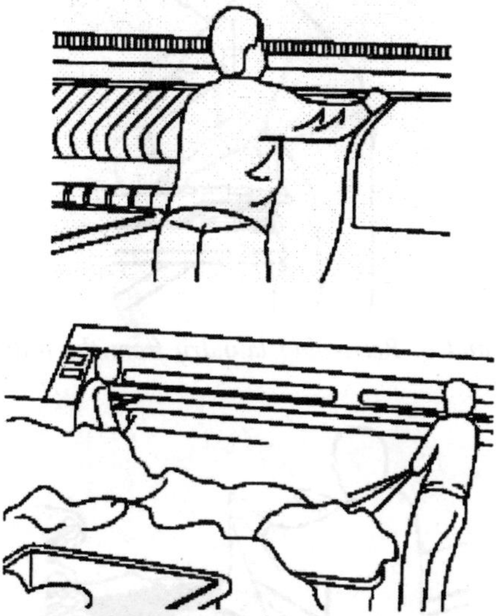

Figures 6 and 7. Feeding the rolling dryer

As an example, to feed the roller dryer with small laundry such as pillow cases (Figure 6), a worker performs the following tasks:

— reaching for the laundry in the bin (Figure 11)

— unfolding and stretching the laundry

— spreading the laundry on rollers (Figure 6)

Contd . . .

Figures 8 and 9. Retrieving laundry from the rolling dryer

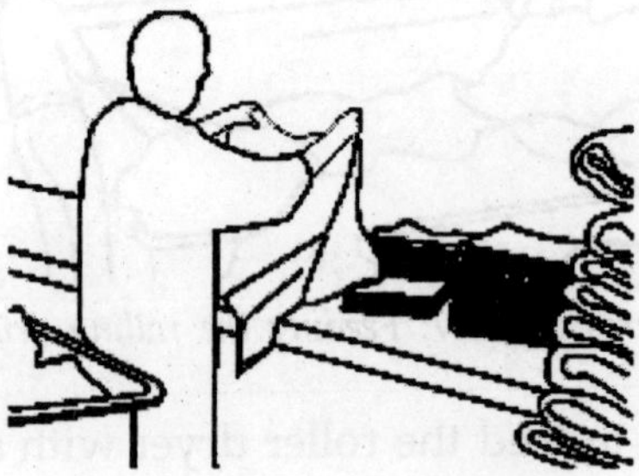

Figure 10. Folding towels

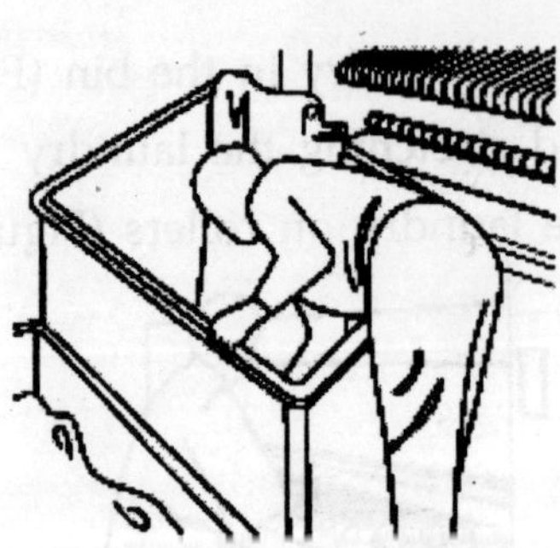

Figure 11. Reaching for the laundry

To feed the dryer with laundry such as bed sheets, two workers form a team (Figure 7). This task involves the following:

— reaching for bedsheets in the bin (Figure 11)
— unfolding the bedsheets
— spreading the bedsheets (Figure 12)
— spreading the bedsheets on rollers

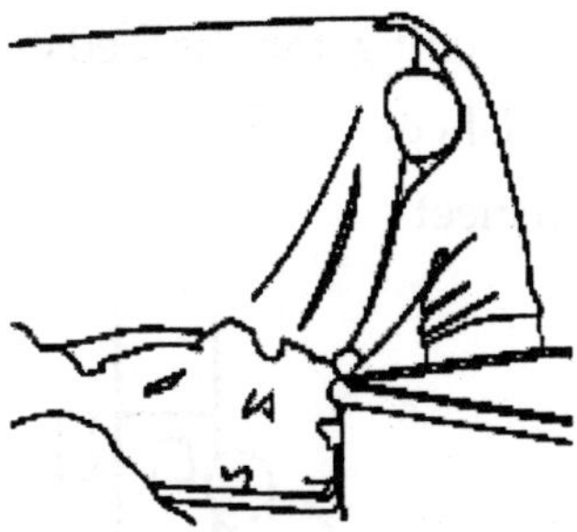

Figure 12. Spreading the laundry

Several aspects of feeding the dryer with both small and large pieces of laundry pose the risks for repetitive motion injuries. Workers are at a high risk for upper arm, neck and shoulder injuries because of limited control over the pace of work, highly repetitious movements (one task lasts approximately 3 to 8 seconds), working with arms at or above shoulder level, and hand manipulation while handling the laundry.

Bending and twisting, reaching forward and upward, and standing in a leaning-forward position contribute to low back pain. Prolonged standing on a hard floor contributes to lower leg discomfort and speeds up the development of muscular fatigue. All of these factors have a compounding effect. In other words, each of them increases the effect of the others.

Retrieving Pieces of Laundry

To retrieve small laundry such as pillow cases from the regular dryer (Figure 8) a worker performs the following tasks:

— reaching forward to pick up the laundry
— folding laundry

To retrieve big pieces of laundry such as bedsheets, which come out of the dryer partially folded (Figure 13), a worker performs the following movements:

— bending and reaching for the bedsheet
— folding the bedsheet
— piling the bedsheet

Figure 13. Retrieving bedsheets

Workers involved in retrieving small pieces of laundry are at risk for repetitive motion injuries. The hazardous conditions are:

— no control over pace of work
— repetitive movements
— constrained work posture
— leaning forward standing position
— reaching forward beyond recommended range
— working with extended arms
— standing on a hard floor

The lack of control over the pace of work, highly repetitious movements, constrained work posture. Neck, shoulders and upper arms are at the highest risk for injuries. Leaning forward, over-reaching and prolonged standing in a restricted position put workers at high risk for low back injury.

Prolonged standing on a hard floor contributes to lower leg discomfort and speeds up the development of muscular fatigue. All of these factors have a compounding effect. In other words, each of them increases the effect of the others. Workers involved in retrieving big pieces of laundry are at risk for repetitive motion injuries, including low back pain. The hazardous conditions are:

— prolonged stooped standing position due to a low work surface

— repetitive movements

— standing on a hard floor

— no control over the pace of work

Contributing factors are prolonged, restricted, and stooped working positions and bending. There is also a risk for injuries of the neck and shoulders. Prolonged standing on a hard floor contributes to lower leg discomfort and speeds up the development of muscular fatigue. All of these factors have a compounding effect. In other words, each of them increases the effect of the others.

Towels are dried in a drum type dryer. Dry towels are placed in a bin and are sorted according to size and then folded (Figure 10). This task involves the following:

— reaching into the bin

— grasping the towels

— folding the towels

— piling the towels according to size

Involved in Folding Towels

Workers performing this task are at risk for repetitive motion injuries, including low back pain. The hazardous conditions are:

— continuously bending and twisting

— working with extended arms

— standing on a hard floor

Folding towels puts workers at risk for neck and shoulder injuries. Bending and twisting pose the risk for back injuries. Prolonged standing on a hard floor contributes to lower leg discomfort and low back pain.

Continual twisting and reaching while working with extended arms can contribute to the development of repetitive motion injuries. However, the risk for such injuries while folding towels is somewhat lower when drying and folding of bedsheets and pillow cases. Some control over the pace of work and some flexibility in the working postures are responsible for the reduced risk. We can see how improve the operations in hotel laundry facility:

In the laundry processing plant, the sorting and washing operations are typically manual material handling tasks. These tasks pose the risk for low back pain.

Manual material handling cannot be fully eliminated but it is possible to reduce it by reorganising the flow of work. For example, instead of sorting towels and linen before loading them into the bins, it would be preferable to load the laundry in the bins directly from the pile under the chute. This would eliminate handling the same laundry twice.

Further improvements of working conditions can be achieved by reducing stressful body movements while handling the laundry. Shortening the laundry chute (pipe) through which laundry is dropped would create more space so that the laundry would not compress against the pipe itself. As a consequence, the sorting of the laundry would require less pulling force.

To reduce bending while reaching for the laundry at the bottom of the bins, it would be advisable to use different types of bins. For example, a bin with one side that opens mounted on a moveable tilt/lift table (Figure 14). To reduce pulling and pushing while manoeuvring the bins full of laundry, it would be advisable to use lighter bins with wheels designed for hard floors. In addition, the bins should be maintained regularly with particular attention to the wheels.

Figure 14. Tilt-lift table

Working in the sorting and washing areas requires standing on a concrete floor. Since the application of anti-fatigue matting is not practical, workers should wear shoes that provide good cushioning or they should use proper inserts to lessen the stress on the feet and on the lower back.

The overall workload, poor layout of the work station, improper design of the laundry bins and the repetitiveness of the work are the major risk factors for repetitive motion injuries in the drying and folding job.

Providing bins with one side that opens on elevating devices would reduce bending and other awkward body positions while reaching for towels at the bottom of the bins. To reduce awkward body positions such as reaching above shoulder level while feeding the dryer, it would be advisable to use a platform. Narrowing the counter that separates the worker from the dryer would reduce reaching forward.

To reduce awkward body positions such as reaching above shoulder level while retrieving pillow cases from the dryer, it would be advisable to use a platform (Figure 15). Narrowing the counter that separates the worker from the dryer would reduce reaching forward. Workers should have a sit/stand stool available to rest between tasks. Also, a foot bar to allow the worker to switch the weight of the body from one foot to the other should be made available.

Figure 15. Standing on a platform while retrieving laundry

Partially folded bedsheets coming out of the dryer should be collected in a basket (Figure 16) so that when completing the folding operation, a worker can use a counter of appropriate height and reduce excessive bending.

To reduce discomfort due to prolonged standing while folding towels, anti-fatigue matting should be used. Also, a saddle chair and a foot bar should be provided.

To further reduce the stress on the body due to prolonged standing, it would be advisable to use sit/stand devices (Figure 17). If it is not practical to sit while performing the task, workers should use these devices between tasks.

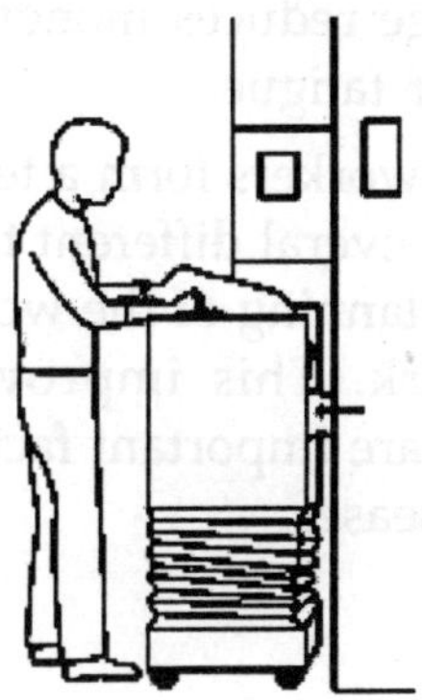

Figure 16. Collecting bedsheet in a basket

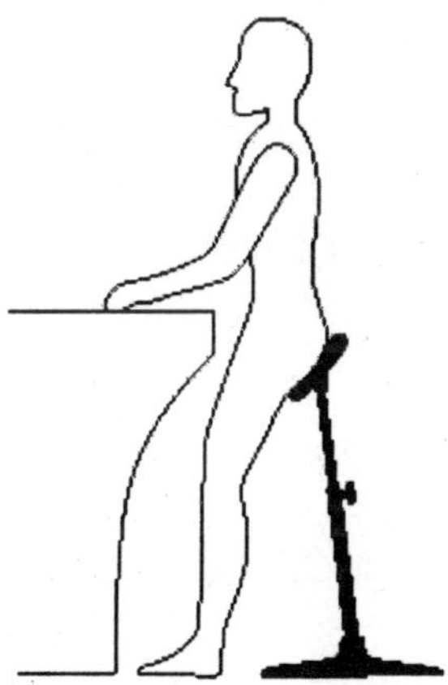

Figure 17. A sit-stand saddle chair

One of the main risk factors for repetitive motion injuries in the laundry is the repetitiveness of the work. To change the repetitive patterns of work, we need to do different tasks. Job rotation and team work are two options that allow workers to vary tasks.

Job rotation requires workers to move between different tasks at fixed or irregular periods of time. Workers in the laundry cannot fully benefit from job rotation because all the tasks are similar in nature. Still, the feeling of change reduces monotony and slows down the development of fatigue.

In team work, workers form a team and each member of the team shares several different tasks. The whole team is involved in the planning of the work. The team controls all aspects of work. This improves attitude and job satisfaction, which are important factors in the prevention of occupational diseases.

2

Essential Tips for Laundry Management

In the old days laundry was done with soaps, scrub boards, wash tubs and lots of elbow grease. Today's advanced washing machines, hitech detergents and laundry additives make wash days easier and more successful, especially with the array of fabrics used in contemporary clothing. The laundry basics, however, haven't changed and are more important than ever. Here is a quick refresher to help get sparkling- clean results, washload after washload.

Laundry Sorting

Proper laundry sorting is important to prevent laundry problems like dye transfer from one garment to another, shrinking clothes and unsightly lint accumulations over the rest of the wash. Follow care labels, if there is any doubt about proper care. Sort laundry loads according to:

— *Colour*

  — Whites and pastels together

  — Same colour brights

  — Dark colours

Multicoloured items with lots of white background are best washed separately first. If colors don't bleed or run, then they can be washed with other items in the future.

— *Fabric and construction*

  — Separate delicate or lightweight fabrics from heavier items

  — Separate lint givers (terrycloth) from lint catchers (corduroy)

Loosely knit sweaters, lingerie or items with delicate trim require gentle care and need to be separated from heavier items like jeans. Different fabrics need different laundry care- be sure to read and follow the care label directions.

— *Degree of Soil*

  — Heavily soiled work or play clothes should be washed separately from lightly soiled laundry

  — Wash diapers and soiled bed linens separately to avoid contaminating other clothes.

Taking an extra minute to check clothing prior to washing can save serious problems later. Pockets with crayons, tissues, lipstick or other surprises can leave laundry streaked with shredded tissues or a rainbow of stains. Before washing:

— Empty pockets

— Shake out loose dirt from cuffs

— Close zippers and other fasteners to prevent snagging and fabric tearing

— Mend rips or tears before laundering, to prevent further damage

— Tie strings and sashes loosely to avoid tangling

— Remove belts, pins, trim or ornaments that are not washable

Laundry Products

Successful laundry results start with the right laundry products. Here's a checklist of laundry essentials:

Detergents

Detergents work to effectively remove soil and prevent lint and soil from redepositing on clothes. Follow directions for the proper amount and measure, don't guess. Extra detergent is needed for large loads, extremely dirty clothes, or hard water. Likewise less detergent is required for small loads, lightly soiled clothes, or soft water. More laundry problems are usually caused from using too little detergent rather than using too much.

— Granular detergents are recommended for hard water conditions and when loads contain mud or clay soil.

— Liquid detergents are especially good for cold water washing and for cleaning greasy, oily stains.

— Detergent with bleach combines colour-safe bleach with either granular or liquid detergent.

— Detergent with fabric softener both cleans and softens laundry.

Bleach

You can keep washables whiter and brighter longer when bleach is used in every washload. Choosing the right bleach is easy:

— Household liquid bleach, identified by the words "sodium hypochlorite" in the ingredient listing is the only bleach that disinfects. It is also the most effective bleach for stain removal and whitening. This is the bleach of choice for whites and colourfast garments. It pays to do the bleach-safe test when you think a garment should be bleachable. Clorox laundry studies confirm that about 52 percent of all washables are actually safe with household liquid bleach. Other laundry studies show how liquid bleach is safe for fabrics, when used as directed. This bleach does not wear down fabrics any more than detergent alone, washload after washload.

— Colour-Safe Bleach is, quite simply, a bleach that is safe to use on washable, coloured clothes. These bleaches, available in powder and liquids, remove stains and help keep colors bright. The powdered bleaches also have enzymes to break up tough protein stains, which is why they make an excellent presoak. A colour-safe bleach is not a diluted bleach. The gentle bleaching action in liquids is from hydrogen peroxide. Powders commonly use sodium perborate. These colour-safe bleaches also have optical brighteners. This ingredient is like an invisible layer on fabrics. It reflects light, making colors appear brighter and whites whiter.

Adding bleach to washer: Many washing machines today are equipped with convenient automatic bleach dispensers for household liquid bleach. If a washer is not equipped with a liquid bleach dispenser follow either of these two methods:

— For maximum cleaning results...

   — Add detergent as washer fills, then add clothes.

   — After machine has agitated for 5 minutes, add household liquid bleach that has been diluted in 1 quart of water. Avoid pouring mixture directly onto clothes.

Always use this method when using detergent with bleach products.

— Convenient and effective...

- — While the machine fills with water, pour in liquid bleach and detergent.
- — Once agitation begins, add clothes.

If you think a care label is inaccurate and an item should be bleachable, here's how to test the fabric:

— *Bleach safe test*:

- — Mix 1 tablespoon household liquid bleach with 1/4 cup water.
- — Dab 1 drop of this solution on a hidden part of a fabric such as an inside seam, hemline or cuff. Be sure to test all colors and any decorative trim or ribbing.
- — Wait 1 minute, then blot dry with paper towel. If there is no change, the fabric can be safely washed with household liquid bleach.

Prewash Soil and Stain Removers: These products are formulated to help get clothes stain free. Their special detergents and enzymes penetrate stains and break them up, helping detergents work more effectively to wash stains away.

Fabric Softeners: Fabric Softeners help reduce static cling, minimise wrinkling and soften clothes. Rinse-added softeners are added to the final rinse cycle. These can be added automatically in washers equipped with a fabric softener dispenser. Otherwise, diluted softener must be added manually to the final rinse. Dryer sheets are convenient to use with one sheet added to the dryer along with the clothes.

LAUNDARY CLEANING

Water plays a major role in how clean the laundry is... hardness or softness, level and temperature all affect the laundry process. Soft water aids in the cleaning process, while hard water can create some problems. If water is hard, add a water softener or more detergent than the product label recommends. Both help to soften the water and increase the cleaning power of detergent.

Choosing the proper water level and temperature is vital for best cleaning. Laundry must have ample room to circulate, clean and rinse properly or the dirt will end up back on the clothes. Use a hot water wash for most white fabrics and heavily soiled coloured fabrics. Warm water is recommended for very lightly soiled or brightly coloured garments, and most other laundering needs. With increased concern for energy conversation, many consumers are lowering hot water heater thermostats as well as washing in cooler water. While this saves energy, laundry results are not always satisfactory. For effective cleaning, hot water heaters should be set no lower than 120F, but hotter water up to 140F gives better cleaning results.

Drying Time

Before putting garments into the dryer, shake them out so they are loose, not bunched up. This will allow quicker drying. Always check that stains are removed before drying. Heat can permanently set some stains making them impossible to remove. Avoid overdrying, which can cause shrinking and wrinkling. Remove clothes from the dryer as soon as it shuts off. For maximum drying efficiency, clean the lint filter after each load.

Water temperatures below 65F won't activate some laundry additives and may cause lint, residue, and poor cleaning. Detergent manufacturers and care labels define cold water. as 65- 85F. Some suggestions to maximise cleaning Efficiency

— Presoak and pretreat stains

— Use appropriate bleach.

— Increase the amount of detergent and extend wash time, if possible.

— Don't overload the washer.

CHALLENGES OF LAUNDRY

Household liquid bleach can make a difference in tackling both common and special laundry problems, as well as eliminating bacteria and germs for a safer, cleaner and healthier wash.

Kids Stains

— *Blood*: Rinse in cool water and pretreat with soil and stain remover. Rinse and repeat until stain is gone. Launder in cold water, using appropriate bleach.

— *Grass*: Pretreat stains with soil and stain remover, allow to sit for 5 minutes. Launder in hottest water safe for fabric, using appropriate bleach.

— *Mud*: Allow to dry, then brush off excess mud, Pretreat stain, allow to sit for 5 minutes. Launder in hottest water safe for fabric, using appropriate bleach.

— *Crayon*: To remove crayola stains, the Crayola Company recommends: Place the stained surface down on a pad of paper towels, spray with WD-40, and let stand for a few minutes. Turn the fabric over and spray the other side. Apply liquid dishwashing detergent and work it into the stained area. Replace towels as they absorb the stain. Wash in hot water with laundry detergent and bleach for about 12 minutes (use "heavy soiled" setting if there is no minute timer on your machine), and rinse in warm water.

— *Fingerpaints, ballpoint ink & felt tip markers*: Pretreat stains and launder in hottest water safe for the fabric, using appropriate bleach. Permanent markers may be impossible to remove.

— *Baby Formula*: Soak in cool water using a presoak product. Launder in hottest water safe for fabric, using appropriate bleach

— *Diaper stains, vomit Rinse off soils*: Launder in hottest water safe for fabric with appropriate bleach, To kill bacteria that contribute to diaper rash, add liquid bleach to the wash cycle.

— *Vitamins, liquid pain relievers*: Pretreat and let sit for 5 minutes. Launder in hottest water possible, using appropriate bleach.

Food Stains

— *Beverages*: Sponge promptly with cold water or soak in cold water. Pretreat and launder in hottest water safe for fabric, using appropriate bleach.

— *Egg, milk & milk products*: Rinse in cool water and pretreat. Rinse and repeat, if necessary. launder in cold water, using appropriate bleach.

— *Chocolate, fruit flavoured drinks, gravy, juices, tomato products Soak in cool water*: Pretreat, wait a few minutes, then wash in hottest water possible safe for the fabric, using appropriate bleach.

— *Mayonnaise, mustard, salad dressing*: Pretreat, launder in hottest water safe for fabric, using appropriate bleach.

— *Oil and grease, perspiration and deodorant*: Pretreat and launder in hottest water safe for fabric, using appropriate bleach.

Tips for Stain Removal

— Treat stains early. Fresh stains are easier to remove than old ones.

— Rub stain remover gently onto garment and wash in hottest water safe for fabric.
— Check that stains are gone before machine drying or ironing. Heat can set some stains permanently.
— If stain remains, pretreat and wash again.
— Some stains, including inks, dyes, and rust may be permanent.

Special Concerns

Kitchen

Dish towels, cloths, and sponges really get around the kitchen, and are a breeding ground for germs. In a recent study of kitchen bacterial contamination, 20 percent of the dish cloths and 12 percent of the sponges contained salmonella, a leading cause of food-borne illness.

Since food-borne bacteria can double in number every 20 minutes in some conditions, it's important to wash towels and sponges often in hot water and liquid bleach. A convenient way to disinfect dish cloths and sponges in-between washings, is to soak for 5 minutes in a solution of:

— cup household liquid bleach
— gallon warm water

Ideally, kitchen surfaces should be disinfected daily.

Disinfect Laundry

Liquid bleach has a long history of use in places where disinfection is critical such as in hospitals, nursing homes and restaurants. At home, regular laundering with liquid bleach may help reduce the spread of disease-causing bacteria and viruses. Liquid bleach eliminates disease-causing organisms and provides a safer, healthier home environment. This is especially important when laundering soiled bedding, clothing and diapers from those incontinent. Using liquid bleach for cleaning, disinfecting and removing stains is important for a greater sense of comfort as well as cleanliness.

S.O.S. (Save Our Stuff!)

The removal of smoke odor from clothes following a fire is a challenging task. Sulphuric acid, carbon, and other components smoke become trapped between fabric fibers and must be eliminated. The greater the severity of the smoke damage, the more difficult to restore. Separate washable items from those that must be dry cleaned. Separate heavily smoke damaged items from those less severe.

Dry cleaning, frequently suggested by many insurance companies, is not always effective in removing stains and odors. A recent study on smoke damage and fabrics representing the majority of today's apparel fabrics demonstrated the effectiveness of home laundering. The study showed that five launderings with detergent in combination with liquid bleach successfully removed visible smoke damage and odors.

Useful smoke damage tips

These procedures are useful in handling smoke damage of textiles:

— Washable textiles with mild smoke damage should be hung outside, at least 3 inches apart. To allow for greater air circulation, do not close fasteners such as zippers or buttons. Fresh air, particularly with at least a light breeze and sunlight are natural partners in helping to remove smoke odor from clothing. An electric fan can be used to supplement the air flow through the clothes. Clothing should be left outside four to eight hours, with repeated airings if smoke odor is still strong.

— Wash items in the hottest water possible safe for the fabric with liquid household bleach (sodium hypochlorite), if not suitable with liquid household bleach then use a colour-safe bleach.

— *Check items for odor*: Usually several washings are needed to fully remove odor. Once odor is eliminated, line dry in the sunlight. Do not dry in the dryer because heat will set any lingering odor.

Presoak procedure

— Use ¼ cup household liquidbleach per gallon of water.

— Submerge entire garment and soak for 5 minutes.

— Rinse and wash according to care label.

Powdered coloursafe Bleach presoak

— Use 1 cup dry bleach pergallon of water.

— Soak 30 minutes or overnight.

When using any bleach as a presoak, be sure to soak the entire garment as well as other sections worn together for best results.

New Care Symbols

Reading labels is an important element to insure an effective wash. By law, manufacturers must place labels on garments, specifying at least one safe cleaning method. When care symbols are used, laundering instructions will include, in order, four symbols—washing, bleaching, drying and ironing.

Drycleaning instructions will use one symbol, a circle. Additional symbols or words Here is a sampling of the new care symbols for washing, bleaching, drying, and ironing.

Problem Solver

Best way to treat unknown stains: Soak the item in cold water for 20 minutes, pretreat and launder with a generous amount of detergent and the hottest water possible for the fabric. If item is bleach-safe and you know the stain is not rust, use liquid bleach. Air dry item until the stain is removed. Machine drying can set the stain and make further removal almost impossible.

Colour bleeding occurs when unstable dyes are used and bleed from one garment to another. Some of the newer garments are overdyed to produce very bright, rich colors resulting in dye removal and/or transfer when laundered. Sorting brightly coloured garments, washing separately and avoiding prolonged contact of damp items before and after laundering helps to minimise this damage. If dye transfer has occurred, pretreat and relaunder in warm water. As a last resort, for whites only, use a commercial colour remover, following package directions.

Eliminate dinginess and Poor Cleaning: Overall dinginess and inadequate cleaning can result from a number of factors. Cleaning results can be improved by:

Proper sorting; pretreating spots, stains and heavily soiled garments

- Using enough detergent
- Using hot enough water suitable for the fabric
- Using the proper water setting on the washer
- Loading the washer loosely
- Using bleach to improve stain removal and overall cleaning results.

Mildew on clothing: If Mildew is not severe, pretreat the stains and launder in the hottest water recommended for the item along with liquid bleach, if appropriate for fabric. For more extensive cases, presoak bleach-safe fabrics in a solution of 1/4 cup liquid bleach per gallon of warm water. Household items and clothes soaked during flooding require disinfecting. Always wear rubber or plastic gloves when handling flood-soaked items. Sort soiled garments as soon as possible, separating washable items from those requiring drycleaning.

For washable items, rinse several times in cold water, soaking heavily soiled items overnight. Presoak heavily soiled items in powdered colour-safe bleach, following package directions. Machine wash using 1-1/2 times the amount of detergent recommended along with bleach in the hottest water possible for the fabric. For drycleanables, consult a professional dry-cleaner.

Laundry Cost Factors

The percentages associated with laundry cost are important to know when trying to evaluate cost. All costs are important, but some are bigger than others. Here are some accepted ranges for laundry cost: Labour 35-55 percent, Linen Replacement 15-25 percent, Energy 10-15 percent, Chemicals 5-10 percent, Indirect 5-20 percent.

Labour Cost

Cost of wages and benefits to employees. A manager should review procedures and training in order to optimise the output per employee, commonly referred to as pounds per operator hour. Knowing the productivity of employees, and what it should be for the type of laundry and equipment in use is critical to controlling labour cost.

Cost of Linen Replacing

Cost of replacing linens to a predetermined par-stock. A manger should evaluate the quality and life of linens. This can include theft, normal wear, and intensity of wash formulas, rejects, and overall handling procedures by housekeeping personnel, as well as the laundry staff. Buying the right quality and controlling its use can be beneficial to reducing replacement cost.

Laundry today is the source for new career opportunities, selling & buying of new and used equipment. And of course, we want to provide you with information on a monthly basis.

Cost of Energy

Cost of water, sewer, electricity, and gas A manager can evaluate equipment efficiency in wash formulas—full loads, proper temperatures, and cycle times—and see that all are balanced to deliver high quality with a low re-wash percentage. Properly utilising dryers with full loads, correct temperatures and times helps control finishing costs. This is a variable cost that is often overlooked, but is a real cost that should be analysed closely.

Cost of Chemical Use

Cost of all supplies used to clean linens A manager should review all options to take advantage of technology that can deliver the benefits of controlling cost in the above areas as well as the chemistry itself. The chemistry used can dramatically affect other variable cost, so close scrutiny is well advised.

Cost of Miscellaneous Works

Cost of maintenance, depreciation, equipment, and laundry

floor space. A manager may be able to help control maintenance by maximising equipment efficiency and using preventive maintenance. Reducing total hours of operation can reduce cost associated with room and space by cutting lighting, heating, or air conditioning cost, etc.

Manage Laundry Function

An important part of marketing a hotel is maximising repeat business. Linen is one of the physical items with which guests come in the most contact. It should look good and be well maintained. This is one item that an economy lodging property can use to set itself above its competition in perceived value relatively inexpensively. This can be done in several ways.

The first is in the weight and size of the terry. Imported ROL (run of the loom) or seconds should never be used. Terry should be either a quality domestic or a first class import. The higher the cotton content the better. The size and weight should be similar to what a person might use at home. Nobody uses a ten inch square 12 ounce per dozen wash cloth at home. Likewise, nobody has an 18 inch wide bath towels that you can see through at home.

Linen (sheeting and terry) standards for limited service economy lodging are as follows: All sheets are T-180 Percale and 110" long. There are 108" sheets, but hey don't tuck in as well and the guests' toes can feel the mattress! Bath towels 24" x 48" or 50"—(10.5 lbs. per dozen); Hand Towels 16"x27"—3.0; Wash Cloths 12"x12" - 1.0 and Bath mats 20"x30" - 7.0; Shower Curtains are washable nylon.

We also have another unusual standard for this market segment: all linen is beige. This costs about 5.0% more than white but has several advantages. The first is that bleach isn't used which results in two costs savings:

one doesn't have to buy bleach, and because bleach isn't used, the linen lasts much longer and wears and feels better. The cotton in white linen breaks down after many bleachings and begins to appear gray as the cotton is washed out, leaving only the synthetic backing.

The second advantage is that the beige linen just looks better and less institutional. The guest room and bathroom have a more residential feeling. A smaller advantage is that stains do not show up as readily. The disadvantage is that the terry is stolen at a slightly higher rate. On balance, overall, beige linen provides a cost savings and a marketing advantage.

The room attendant should note stained lined when she removes it from the guest room separate it so that it will be noticed right away when it arrives in the laundry area later. Spotting and stain removal instruction and supplies should be readily available in the laundry. Regular soiled laundry should be separated by type, percal, terry, and others such as spreads, etc. Within those groups the heavily soiled laundry should also be separated so that all laundry is not washed with the heaviest concentrations of chemical and suffer the extra wash cycles. If more than one colour of linen is used, white should be separated from other colours if bleach is to be used on the white linen.

Linen should never be placed on the floor by the room attendant or the laundry staff. The floor soils linen and contributed to wear. Unsealed concrete some other surfaces will stain or change the pH (Acidity/alkalinity) of the linen at the point of contact. Sort linen into laundry carts. For the sake of the people working in the laundry and your workers' compensation premiums, use spring loaded inserts in your laundry carts. They will raise the linen as the cart is emptied so your staff does not have to bend or stoop as much. High bottom carts whose sides are about even with the doors of your of washers and dryers are good for moving linen from washers to dryers.

Washers should generally be loaded fully but not with linen crammed in them. Use the minimum cycle setting to do the job. Don't waste chemicals, energy, wear and tear on the washer and linen by overdoing the wash cycles. Your laundry supply vendor, if reputable, will help you make sure your machines and chemicals are set properly and review the operation with responsible supervisors for no extra charge. They will also test your water and inspect your machines as part of their service. If they won't do it, and help you keep a written record of it, change vendors.

When the wash is complete, move the laundry to the dryers as soon as possible. Typically it takes twice the capacity of the washer, as measured in pounds, to do the drying. With this mix of equipment, drying time will be approximately the same as washing time, linen will tumble loosely, and dry out without being beat up as much in the dryer. Be sure to use the proper cool down cycle and remove the linen as soon as possible to reduce wrinkling.

If you have an opportunity to redo your laundry area because replacement or additional equipment is needed to take advantage of this to arrange the equipment so that labour expense is minimised by lessening the necessary motions in moving things are minimised.

Linen should be folded immediately and allowed to rest overnight. The rest allows linen to iron itself and become wrinkle-free. Most of dirty linen complaints come from what the guests believe is dirty because of the wrinkles. The second biggest cause is hair, which seems to be a result of overloading washers and/or dryers. Resting the linen helps it last longer in terms of usage. The person folding the laundry should watch carefully as s/he folds to observe stains and excessive wear or fraying. Stains can be reworked and fraying can be trimmed sometimes.

It costs money to move linen around in a hotel. It is a labour cost which can be controlled. If we purchase a very large cart with shelves from very large hotels, the laundry staff folds laundry and immediately places it in the cart. The cart is then used to deliver clean linen to the room attendants' carts around the hotel. Room attendants' carts are also brought to the laundry each night for cleaning and stocking by an afternoon laundry person. This reduces labour cost and enables us to control the stocking and appearance of the carts.

An adequate linen inventory is essential for the efficient operation of a housekeeping department. Having to strip rooms to collect up soiled linen in order to begin washing so there will be clean linen for the rooms is very wasteful in labour expense and precludes letting the linen rest. Having at least two and a half times the linen necessary to set up all the rooms once is called having 2.5 par. This multiple does not apply to mattress pads, bed spreads, shower curtains, pillows, etc. For these items 1.2 to 1.5 par is usually sufficient.

Inventory should be taken monthly and include a count for the linen enroute from your supplier. Subtract the resulting inventory from the 2.5 par and order that quantity. Most items come in dozens and packed a minimum of five dozen to the case. Round up to get full cases. Build up to three par if you have a busy season immediately ahead of you.

If you must order in less than case lots because your hotel is small, order from a reliable supplier who will maintain an inventory that meets your specifications. Typically those storing and shipping unless that case lots still work in even dozens and their charges all include freight. Finally, the laundry and housekeeping areas must be immaculate.

This is not only where you demonstrate to your staff what the standard is for the entire hotel, but also the way you should treat your employees. You want them to have pride in their hotel and their work area. Just because it is out of sight of the guest doesn't mean it can be ignored. Keep the area so that it functions efficiently and you are proud for both your guests and your banker to see it.

3

Responsibilities of Laundry Manager

Laundry manager has large scale supervisory works in holtel industry. An employee in this class is responsible for the efficient and economical operation and maintenance of a high volume laundry engaged in processing linen supplies, uniforms and various items used in a large medical facility. An additional responsibility may include the rendering of technical advice and assistance to a prisoner-operated laundry at a large county penal institution.

Work also includes the supervision of a central linen service unit engaged in mending, repairing and storing laundered supply items. The incumbent in this class exercises considerable independent judgment in discharging the duties required while receiving only general direction from an administrative superior who periodically checks operational efficiency through review of production reports and cost records. Supervision is exercised through subordinate laundry foreman over all assigned personnel by determining quality and quantity production controls and through inspection of work in process.

Assigns, supervises and reviews the work of a large number of laundry employees engaged in receiving, washing, ironing, packaging and delivering laundry to various departments; consults with subordinate supervisory personnel regarding work schedules and problems. Trains new employees in correct and efficient methods of hand and machine laundry operations, and inspects their work closely until duties are thoroughly learned. Supervises through a subordinate supervisor, sewing and mending services for the hospital.

Assigns and reassigns personnel in order to meet emergency situations caused by vacation schedules, illness and vacancies in the units; maintains records of time worked by employees; maintains records of production, supplies used, and other costs, and prepares and submits reports on costs and efficiency of laundry and related operations. Observes, analyses and revises laundry and sewing room schedules and assignments in order to maintain efficient operation in accordance with varying work load requirements.

Maintains a stock of supplies including soaps, bleaches, starches and other standard laundry supplies; makes or arranges for the making of minor repairs and adjustments to the laundry machines and equipment and to sewing machinery and equipment; sees that machinery is adequately oiled and greased; recommends equipment replacement and writes purchase specifications. Insures proper training of new employees in hand and machine operations; periodically inspects their work for adherence to work methods.

Classification Factors

Supervision Received—Level D: "Under general direction..." Employees at this level are usually in charge of a large and important organisational unit. They plan and carry out assignments with little supervision. They report regularly to a superior, usually by means of occasional conferences, to discuss work progress or new problems which require advice from above. This designation will pertain to classes with a high order of independence.

Difficulty—LEVEL B: Average... Where the employee is confronted with a variety of duties susceptible to different methods of solution which, in turn, places a correspondingly higher demand upon resourcefulness and concentration. Positions which require the analysis and evaluation of raw data and the rendering of conclusions would, in many instances, fall into this category.

Complexity—LEVEL C: Work is of a standardised nature that may involve a variety of duties. Analytical thought becomes more important at this level due to increased data and changing situations. Tasks usually have several steps, some of which may not be directly related. Alternatives may exist for processes or methods to be used in solving problems. Workers at this level exercise a moderate amount of independent judgment. Work is controlled by routine review and reporting to or consultation with supervisors. When guidelines exist at this level, they tend to be more complicated or technical in nature requiring careful interpretation.

Consequence of Actions or Decisions—LEVEL D: Consequences of actions or decisions at this level are significant as the work may be rarely if ever reviewed, making errors difficult to detect. Errors may cause major programme failure or a high degree of confusion. Injuries to others due to errors are serious or incapacitating or both and costs due to errors are substantial.

Contacts—LEVEL C: The purpose of the contact is to influence, motivate, conduct interviews, make formal presentations or counsel to achieve common understanding or solutions to problems when the information is sensitive in nature or the individuals or groups are skeptical or uncooperative. Communication techniques and well developed communication skills become an important requirement at this level.

Physical Demands—LEVEL A: The work is predominantly sedentary and requires minimal or negligible physical exertion. The employee is normally seated; however, the nature of the work allows for periods of standing or walking at will.

Environmental Conditions—LEVEL A: The work environment involves normal everyday hazards or discomforts typical of offices, meeting and training rooms, or libraries. Comfortable levels of temperature, ventilation, lighting and sound are inherent in the work environment. Exposure to deviations from pleasant environmental conditions is only occasional. The likelihood of injury is remote.

Supervision/Leadership—LEVEL C: Typically involves limited supervisory responsibility which entails performing as a "first line supervisor" for a small number of employees. Supervision is not the primary responsibility of the job. Responsibility includes training, instructing, scheduling, and reviewing work and recommending hiring and disciplinary actions to a higher level of authority.

Distinguishing Features

Differs from the Laundry Supervisor class in which the work is primarily supervisory in nature. Establishes and reviews procedures and policies for the provision of laundry services; coordinates the collection and distribution of laundry from and to a number of separate units with varying needs and requirements. Directs and manages a multi-operational laundering process; approves safety procedures for the proper use of equipment.

Estimates and projects budgetary costs for new equipment, major repairs, additional personnel and expendable supplies. Coordinates all grievances and disciplinary matters; approves or recommends selection of employees; evaluates the review of employee performance in order to ensure that the personnel function is performed satisfactorily. Plans and coordinates the training the procurement functions of the department in order to facilitate operations.

Knowledge

- Knowledge of occupational hazards in an institutional laundry and of necessary safety precautions.
- Knowledge of the principles and techniques of supervision.
- Knowledge of the principles of inventory control.
- Knowledge of approved methods and practices of laundering linens, uniforms, and other institutional laundry, as well as new techniques or experimental formulas.
- Knowledge of the procedures and policies involved in the efficient management of an institutional laundry.
- Knowledge of various textiles and types of laundry used by institutions, including the most appropriate laundering methods and techniques.
- Knowledge of the principles and practices involved in effectively managing a laundry that provides services to several large institutions with unique laundry requirements
- Knowledge of all phases of the laundry trade, including recent trade in development of equipment, materials, formulas, and procedures.
- Knowledge of the policies and procedures involved in operating a large institutional laundry in a

productive manner, and of the operation and maintenance of equipment and machinery employed in a laundry.

Abilities

— Ability to effectively express ideas orally.

— Ability to maintain and organise filing and record keeping systems.

— Ability to observe and analyse problems in laundry production and to implement changes where necessary to improve efficiency of working conditions.

— Ability to prepare reports of laundry operations, based on the interpretation of detailed records.

— Ability to schedule laundry production to provide a smoother and continuous flow of work through all operations.

— Ability to coordinate laundry services to several large institutions in a manner that provides efficient service to all units.

— Ability to organise, assign, direct and evaluate the work of a large staff of laundry employees who handle a variety of institutional linens, uniforms, and clothing.

— Ability to assess laundry procedures or policies and to make appropriate modification to provide smooth, uninterrupted laundry service to a very large number of units.

— Ability to assess and analyse production, cost, and personnel and equipment performance records and to prepare budget requests and other reports pertaining to continuing or proposed operations.

4

Cleaning and Stain Removal

There are several trade secrets to get rid of the most stubborn stains and smells as well as information on how to care for a hotel. Also included is advice from cleaning experts on keeping a neat and tidy living space.

Acid Cleaners

Acid cleaners can be used to remove tarnish, alkaline discoloration and corrosion from metals; remove hard water deposits from many surfaces; will neutralize alkalis; may have bleaching effects.

Mild Acid Cleaners: *Mild Acid Cleaners* include Lemon Juice (or Citric Acid) and Vinegar (or Acetic Acid). They help dissolve hard water deposits from shower doors, mild rust stains and soap film and remove tarnish from brass and copper. Acids tend to bleach some stains.

Mild Acid Cleaners—Cream of Tartar (or Tartaric Acid): For example if you simmer a solution (1 tablespoons of cream of Tartar in a quart of water and discolorization of aluminum pans, caused by alkalai such as tomato sauce, will tend to disappear.

Strong Acid Cleaners—Oxalic Acid: Used in commercial rust removers to remove iron rust; a weak solution will remove rust stains from tubs and sinks.

Strong Acid Cleaners: Dilute hydrochloric acid, dilute sulfuric acid, muriatic acid and sodium bisulfate. These acids are used in some toilet bowl cleaners and etching compounds. They remove hard water and iron deposits and organic matter.

Abrasive Cleaners

Abrasive Cleaners are mechanical cleaners. They physically scratch off dirt, stains and tarnish via friction as you rub the surface. They are composed of either particles or physical abraders such as sandpaper, steel wool, scrubbing pads, etc. The finer the particle the less are less abrasive and the coarser the particle the more abrasive. Baking soda and salt can be used as abrasives.

Baking soda is finer, less abrasive. Salt more abrasive. Abrasives dull glossy surfaces and change both the reflection from, and texture of, surfaces. They should never be used on mica because they take away top layers making future cleaning eventually impossible.

Mild Abrasives: include fine plastic mesh pads, nylon coated sponges, fine brass wool, rotten-stone and whiting. Mild abrasives are used to scour pots and pans, oven interiors, and drip pans. Use as directed to remove stains on surfaces as furniture, countertops, etc.

Moderate Abrasive: Cleaners include fine pumice and fine steel wool. Steel wool is actually graded from 0000-super fine, 000-extra fine, 00-very fine, 0-fine, 1-medium, 2-medium course and 3-0 course. The finer 00 and finer should be used lightly on pots and pans when needed to remove burned on crusty foods and grease. They are often used on burnt spills in non self cleaning or continuous cleaning oven interiors when they will not come off with other milder cleaners.

Strong Abrasives: include medium and coarse steel wool, metal mesh cloths and balls, metal brushes, coarse pumice, and sand/silica. Use them on barbecue grills and untreated oven racks for stubborn deposits when damage to surface is not important.

ALKALI CLEANERS

Alkali cleaners remove and suspend heavy soil and grease so it can be rinsed away. Alkalis can damage skin and fabrics, corrode and darken aluminum. Most (except baking soda) are toxic if swallowed.

Mild Alkali Cleaners Baking Soda (Sodium bicarbonate): Soak burnt food from pans in solution of 2 tablespoons per quart of warm water. (For heavier or sticky soil spots, sprinkle on damp sponge, rub and rinse; or make paste of soda.) Clean glass, tile, porcelain enamel, stainless steel sinks, chrome, fixtures, fiberglass tubs and showers. Remove coffee and tea stains from dishes. Clean and deodorize refrigerator.

Moderately Strong Alkali Cleaners Ammonia: Use solution of 2 tablespoons per quart of warm water to clean windows, glass, ovens, range burners, greasy surfaces. Use 1 tablespoon per quart warm water to wash painted walls and rinse well. Will remove some water based floor waxes.

Irritating fumes: Can soften paint, especially latex, if too strong. Has a slight bleaching effect. Always use alone because combining ammonia with other cleaners may produce lethal gases.

Moderately Strong Alkali Cleaners Borax: In mild solution, 1 to 2 tablespoons per gallon of warm water to wash sinks, painted walls, etc. Laundering (as diapers) to remove odors and retard bacterial growth.

Moderately Strong Alkali Cleaners TSP (Tri-Sodium Phosphate): Buy at paint stores, especially ones painter use. Is part of some commercial cleaners. Use a solution of 1 tablespoon per gallon warm water to clean painted surfaces, porcelain fixtures, tile- glazed and unglazed. Removes soot and smoke (greasy dirt).

Strong Alkali Cleaners Washing Soda (Sodium carbonate): Uses In hot solution, soak greasy burners, pans; dissolves grease from drains. Is builder for many powdered detergents.

Very Strong Alkali Cleaners Lye (Sodium hydroxide): Uses are to clean grease from drains and open drains. Found in many drain and oven cleaners.

Bleaches

Bleaches can oxidize and remove stains from surfaces and fabrics. Bleaches may also be used to lighten stains in wood as well as remove the colour naturally in woods such as mahogany.

Mild Bleaches: Sodium Perborate (an ingredient in commercial all purpose bleaches) and Hydrogen Peroxide. A solution will help lighten stains on surfaces such as plastic laminate, etc.

Strong Bleaches: Chlorine Bleach (Sodium hypochlorite). Removes stains. Disinfects toilet bowls, trash cans, other surfaces.

Wood Bleaches: Oxalic Acid, 2 part component wood bleaches . Removes colour and stain from wood. Opens pores of wood to help accept new stain.

Commercial Cleaners

Commercial cleaners are normally made from a combination of one or more of the other types of cleaner family: acids, alkalis, abrasives, bleaches, detergents, and solvents. Most are low sudsing detergents or alkaline-based cleaners. They often contain extra ingredients that are more effective for certain cleaning jobs. For example, some all-purpose household cleaners with petroleum based solvents dissolve grease better. Always read label and follow directions and cautions.

Powdered Cleaners: Dissolve in water; use to clean large surface areas such as painted walls, woodwork and washable floors.

Liquid Cleaners: Are diluted in water and often used for same cleaning jobs as powders. Full strength many make good spot removers.

Aerosol and Liquid Sprays: Use full strength and wipe dry. Usually require no rinsing. For touch-up cleaning and spot removal.

Detergents

Neutral detergents are pH 7 meaning neither acidic nor alkaline.

Mild Detergents - Hand Dish washing Liquid Detergent: Mild detergents have surfactants that dissolve dirt and grease; use in solution of warm to hot water to clean washable surfaces such as counter-tops, appliances, fixtures, floors.

Moderately Strong Detergents - Laundry Detergents Uses: Has both surfactant and builder, so dissolves heavier soil and grease; use in a solution of warm to hot water to clean washable surfaces where a stronger detergent is safe. Use the smallest amount of detergent that will do the job. Low sudsing types are easier to rinse off.

Solvent Cleaners

Solvent cleaners are readily available and are often used to dissolve household soil. The solvent is often the medium the stain or soil goes into to facilitate its removal.

Water is a universal solvent because it will dissolve most kinds of soils except oils. Alkalis, acids, bleaches or detergents are added to water to chemically react with specific soils and loosen them so they are removed with the water. Prompt sponging with water (if material is water safe) will remove many stains without adding chemicals.

Organic Solvents: Acetone, Denatured Alcohol, Petroleum Distillates including kerosene, mineral spirits, naphtha, dry cleaning fluid, and turpentine are used to remove greasy soil, or stains that will not dissolve in water; or used for cleaning surfaces that would be damaged by water. Some remove waxes, wood finishes, and oil-base paint. Many are used in polishes, waxes, spot removers, rug cleaners, degreasers, and all purpose household cleaners.

Quick and Easy Stain Removal

In most families stain removal is a necessary part of clothing care. Quick and cautious stain removal keeps clothes in wearable condition for a longer time and thus helps reduce clothing costs. This bulletin explains how to remove many stains from washable fabrics using easily available laundry supplies.

Fiber Content Labels

You know if a fabric is washable by reading the care label. If the label has warnings such as "do not use chlorine bleach," then you cannot safely use liquid chlorine bleach in stain removal.

Clothing manufacturers are required to tell you the recommended care procedure on a "permanent care label." These labels often appear at the neckline of garments, but sometimes they are in a side seam. These labels tell if the manufacturer recommends hotel laundering or dry-cleaning for routine care of the clothing.

A recommendation for dry-cleaning may relate to the component parts of the garment such as interfacings and trim, rather than to the basic fiber content of the garment. Tailored clothes of wool are often "dry-clean only" while wool sweaters are often "hand washable."

Hang tags or other labels on clothing tell the fiber content. If you understand fiber characteristics, this information can help you decide about the best stain removal procedure. For example, wool or silk can be severely damaged by liquid chlorine bleach, so this bleach should be avoided.

Hang tags may also tell about fiber finishes such as soil release or durable press that are not visible on clothing but can make stain removal easier or more difficult. For example, oily stains bond more firmly with durable press fabrics than with untreated fabrics, making removal more difficult.

Dry-clean Only Label

The procedures described here do not apply to garments labelled dry-clean only. Clothing labelled "dry-clean" or "professionally dry-clean" should be taken to the cleaners promptly. The fiber content of the clothing and the type of stain should be identified for the cleaner. Even professional cleaners cannot remove all stains. The cleaner will usually warn you if the stain cannot be removed, but sometimes this is difficult to predict. Dye stains on coloured fabrics are an example of stains that may not be completely removed.

Synthetic fibers such as acrylic, nylon, olefin, polyester, and blends of these fibers or cottons with permanent-press finishes are tough and durable, but have a special attraction for oil stains. Oil stains should be removed promptly. If oil stains get dryer dried or ironed into fabrics containing these fibers or finishes, removal may be extremely difficult, if not impossible. These oil stains show most on plain medium colours such as light blue or khaki. On the other hand, if treated quickly, oil stains usually can be easily removed.

Synthetic fiber fabrics are also heat sensitive. These fabrics shrink and melt in high temperatures. They can get more-or-less "permanent" wrinkles in the spin-cycle of a washing machine set for a hot-water wash, or from an over-crowded dryer that has run too long. Steam pressing can sometimes remove heat-set wrinkles, but the melting temperature of the fibers is so close to the temperature needed to iron out wrinkles that pressing is tedious and must be done carefully to avoid melting and creating holes. The restored garment may fit differently because of the heat shrinkage.

It is easy to prevent wrinkling in washable blends and permanent press clothes:

— avoid overloading the washer; clothes should move freely,

— be sure the washer is set for "warm" not "hot" water temperature or for the "permanent press" cycle,

— dry on permanent press setting,

— remove from dryer at end of cycle; do not overdry,

— hang on hanger; temporary wrinkles generally "elax" or fall out in a few hours.

Fabrics containing-vinyl or natural rubber will be damaged by most oil solvents. Oil solvents tend to remove the plasticizer in vinyl film fabrics, making them stiff.

Olefins may be damaged by perchloroethylene solvent, but are resistant to trichloroethylene and fluorocarbon dry-cleaning solvents. Acetate fabrics will dissolve in fingernail polish remover (acetone). Triacetate and modacrylic fabrics can be damaged by acetone or paint thinners. Silk, wool, and other hair fibers, such as camel or cashmere, will dissolve in fresh liquid chlorine bleach.

Dilute solutions of liquid chlorine bleach will cause permanent yellowing and stiffening of wool fibers and usually cause weakening and colour loss in silk. Cellulosic fibers, such as cotton, linen, rayon, and ramie, will be weakened by repeated exposure to dilute solutions of liquid chlorine bleach, but bleaches can be safely used on cellulosic fibers for purposes of stain removal. Undiluted bleach can weaken fabrics so that they tear or wear out more quickly.

Contrasting Colours or Trim

Many garments are designed with dark fabrics and white trim or white fabrics and bright coloured trim such as red piping. When these fabrics are labelled washable, people often complain that the colours have "run." The white shirt becomes streaked with pink from the red trim.

Sometimes this problem can be resolved by rewashing the garment in a heavy-duty detergent with warm or hot water. The excess dye that was not permanently in the trim is not likely to be very firmly deposited in its new location either, and sometimes a simple repeat washing will rinse it away. Sometimes bleaching will help, but often the bleach will change the colour of the trim and further change the appearance of the garment.

Since there are no regulations about colour-fastness labelling, there is little that consumers can do when they have problems with colour-fastness except complain to the manufacturer or retailer who sold the goods. As long as care labelling procedures have been carefully followed, most reputable businesses will respond to your complaint in a positive way. Although it may cramp your style, a way to avoid these problems is to not buy clothing with extreme colour contrasts.

The following general procedures apply to nearly all stains. Fresh stains are much easier to remove than old ones, so take care of stains promptly.

— Blot up any excess liquid with a clean white cloth, paper, or other towels. Remove excess solids by gentle scraping or chipping with a dull knife or metal spatula. With some solids such as heavy amounts of surface mud removal may be easier after the stain has dried. Excess can be brushed off before the clothing is submerged for washing.

— Avoid rubbing the stained area with a linty terry towel or a dark-coloured cloth. You may complicate the problem.

— Never rub a fresh stain with bar soap. Soap sets many stains.

— Decide if the fabric is washable or drycleanable. If drycleanable, take to the cleaners as soon as possible (within 24 to 48 hours).

— Do not try to treat suede, leather, or fur. Professional cleaners are needed for these items, and even some professionals do not offer this service.

— Avoid using hot water on stains of unknown origin. Hot water can set protein stains such as milk, egg, or blood.

— Test stain removal agents on a seam or hidden area of the garment to be sure it does not affect the colour or finish of the fabric before starting on the stain.

— Avoid excessive rubbing unless fabric is tough and durable. Rubbing can spread the stain and damage the fiber, finish, or colour.

— Do not iron or press stained fabrics. Heat will set most stains.

— Check laundry for stains before washing. Many stains need pretreatment.

— Inspect wet laundry before drying to be sure stain has been removed. If a stain is still evident, do not dryer dry. The heat of drying will tend to make the stain more permanent.

— Wash heavily soiled items separately. During laundering soil is broken into smaller particles and can be redeposited on cleaner clothing if insufficient detergent is used, water temperature is too, low, washing time too long, or washer is overloaded with too many clothes.

Spot Treatment Technique

A spot treatment confines the stain to a small area and keeps it from spreading. This method is sometimes called "sponging." For spot treatment you need a supply of absorbent material such as, clean rags or paper towels, and a drycleaning solvent, spot remover, or aerosol pretreatment spray.

Follow these steps:

— Pad the working surface with clean rags or paper towels that can be stained as you work.

— Place the stained area or spot on the garment face-down over the padded surface.

— Dampen a small white cloth with solvent.

— Use the dampened cloth to pat the stain from the wrong side. Feather the edges of the stain working from the outside toward the center to keep the stained area from getting larger.

— As the stain transfers to the absorbent material beneath, move it to a different place on the absorbent material so the stain has a clean place to exit into.

— Repeat this procedure until all traces of stain are gone. Launder to remove any ring that might be left by the solvent.

Chemical Solvents and Supplies

Supplies needed for stain removal can usually be found in grocery, drug, general merchandise, or paint stores. Many commercially available products have proprietary formulas that are protected by patent rights and not available to the public. Ingredients listed on labels for safety purposes can help you decide if the product will be useful for the stain removal task- you have to do. There is no miracle product that will remove all stains.

Detergents

— Heavy-duty liquid detergents (Era, Fab, Grease Relief, Tide, Wisk)
— Light-duty liquid detergents (Delicare, Ivory, Lux,Woolite)
— Powdered detergents (Amway, Cheer, Dash, Oxydol, Sears, Tide)

Bleaches

— Hydrogen peroxide
— Powdered all-fabricc bleaches (sodium perborate) (Biz, Borateem, Clorox 2; Purex, Snowy)
— Liquid all-fabric bleaches (Snowy, Vivid)
— Liquid chlorine bleach (sodium hypochlorite) (Clorox, Hi-lex, Purex)
— Liquid chlorine bleaches have a limited shelf-life. If your bleach is more than six months old and has no effect on stains, it may need to be replaced with fresh bleach.

— To test for colourfastness to liquid chlorine bleaches, mix I tablespoon of bleach with 1/4 cup of water. Use an eyedropper to put a drop of this solution on a hidden seam or pocket edge inside the garment. Let it stand two minutes, then blot dry. If there is no colour change it is safe to use the product. Powdered bleach packages have directions for doing colourfastness tests.

Pretreatment products

— Aerosol sprays-petroleum-based solvent (Clorox, Shout, Spray'n Wash)

— Pump-type sprays—detergent based (Clorox, Shout, Spray'n Wash)

Absorbent materials

— Clean white cloths

— Paper towels (white)

— Sponges (white or neutral coloured)

Odor-reducing agents

— Activated charcoal

— Calcium carbonate

— Soda

Safety Precautions

While many stain removal, chemicals and bleaches are commonly used around the hotel, they are still dangerous. Some are flammable; others are toxic. Here are some rules to keep in mind regarding their use:

— Store stain removal materials out of the reach of children. Do not store with food products.

— Read all label directions and warnings. Store chemicals in their original containers so label directions are available in case of an accident.

— Use all chemicals and commercial stain removal product according to label recommendations.

— Avoid getting the chemicals on your skin. Some are easily absorbed.

— Use drycleaning solvents and other chemicals in a well-ventilated room. Toxic fumes can cause illness.

— Do not use solvents near an open flame or electrical outlet.

— Seal containers so that fumes can't escape.

— Never mix stain removal materials together (bleach and ammonia together form toxic fumes).

CLASSIFICATION OF STAINS

The system used here in classifying stains for removal from washable fabrics is not the only one that has been used. Other books or sources may suggest different methods that also may work. The purpose here is to describe at least one method that should give good results using readily available consumer products or supplies if used correctly.

This stain classification system starts with stains that require similar treatment and are easiest to remove if treated promptly and correctly. Stains that require two-step or special treatment are listed last.

Protein Stains

Soak in cold water. Launder.

— Baby food

— Milk

— Baby formula
— Mucous
— Blood
— Cheese sauce
— Mud
— Cream
— Pudding
— Egg
— Urine
— Feces
— Vomit
— Gelatin
— White glue; school paste
— Ice cream

Fresh protein stains can be removed by soaking and agitating in cold water before washing. These stains contain other ingredients besides protein, but it needs treatment first. If hot water is used first, it cooks the protein, causing coagulation between the fibers in the yarns of the fabric, making the stains more difficult to remove. If protein stains are dried or old, scrape or brush off crusted matter (if any), then soak in cold water using a detergent or an enzyme presoak product.

After treating the stain, launder in warm (not hot) water, rinse, and inspect. If stain remains, soak an additional half-hour, then rewash. Bleach may be necessary if the stain was coloured, such as baby food beets, strawberry gelatin, or ice cream.

Tannin Stains

Do not use soap (bar, flake). Use detergents.

— Alcoholic beverages

— Beer

— Berries (cranberries, raspberries, strawberries)

— Coffee

— Cologne

— Felt-tip water colour pen or washable ink

— Fruit juice (apple, grape, orange)

— Soft drinks

— Tea

— Tomato juice

Fresh tannin stains are usually removed by detergent (not soap) washing in hot water (as safe for fabric) during laundering without any treatment. Use of soap (bar soap, soap flakes, or detergents containing natural soap) will make a tannin stain permanent or at least more difficult to remove. Be sure to check the ingredients list of your detergent for soap. More brands now include it for economic reasons. Old tannin stains may need bleaching for more complete removal.

Oil-based Stains

Use heavy-duty detergent with hot water.

— Automotive oil

— Hair oil

— Bacon fat

— Hand lotion

— Butter/margarine

— Lard

— Car door grease

— Mayonnaise

— Collar/cuff greasy rings
— Salad dressing
— Cooking fats and oils
— Suntan oil or lotion
— Face creams

Oil stains can be removed by pretreatment with a heavy-duty liquid detergent, an aerosol petroleum-based solvent pretreatment spray, or a pump-type detergent-based pretreatment spray. If these products are unavailable, you can use a powdered detergent that is mixed with water to make a runny paste and apply that to the stain.

The heavy-duty liquid detergents or aerosol sprays are more convenient and effective. Work the full-strength heavy-duty liquid detergent into the stain or spray with the pretreatment product, then wash the garment using hot water (if safe for fabric), the recommended amount of detergent for a regular laundry load, rinse, and inspect before drying. Repeat this treatment if removal is incomplete the first time.

Dye Stains

Need detergent wash and bleach as safe, for fabric.

— Cherry, blueberry
— Colour bleeding in wash (dye transfer)
— Felt-tip pen (permanent ink-may not come out)
— Grass
— India ink
— Kool-Aid
— Mercurochrome
— Mustard
— Tempera paint

Dye stains are very difficult to remove. First, pretreat the stain with a heavy-duty liquid detergent, then rinse thoroughly. Soak the stained garment in a dilute solution of all-fabric powdered bleach.

If the stain persists, and the garment is white or colourfast, soak in a dilute solution of liquid chlorine bleach and water. Bleaching damage to coloured garments is irreversible. To decide if a fabric can be bleached safely, use the test described previously. If the stain is not removed in 15 minutes, it cannot be removed by bleaching and further bleaching will only weaken the fabric.

Combination Stains

Two step treatment: (1) Remove oily/waxy portion, (2) Remove dye portion using bleach as safe for fabric. Combination stains contain a variety of ingredients, but these stains usually have an oily/waxy component and a dye or pigment component. Use the procedures recommended for removing oil stains first.

Step 1 procedure depends on whether stain is in Group A or B as follows:

Group A: Spray or sponge with drycleaning solvent (perchloroethylene, trichloroethylene) then rub with heavy-duty liquid detergent before washing.

— Ball-point ink

— Candle wax

— Carbon paper

— Carbon typewriter ribbon

— Crayon

— Eye make-up (mascara, pencil, liner, shadow)

— Floor wax

— Furniture polish

— Lipstick
— Livestock paint
— Pine resin
— Shoe polish
— Tar

Group B: Rub heavy-duty liquid detergent into stain before washing.

— Barbecue sauce
— Calomine lotion
— Catsup or tomato sauce
— Cocoa or chocolate
— Face make-up (powder, rouge, foundation)
— Gravy
— Hair spray

After you've done the procedures above, do step 2-removing dye stains. Start with an all-fabric bleach because it is less damaging to colours and fabrics. Use liquid chlorine bleaches for tough dye stains, if fabrics are colourfast to bleach.

If you don't know what the stain is, its odor, location, and colour may give you a clue. Old oil stains may smell rancid, but appear dry. Food stains are often on the front of garments; perspiration stains around collars and underarms; black grease is often on pants or skirts at car-door latch levels.

Stain colour may be a misleading clue. For example, rust-coloured stains may be coffee, tea, old lemonade stains (carmelized sugar), cosmetics containing benzoil peroxide (which can bleach many colours to look rusty), felt marker, crayon, aged baby formula, or a number of other things. If a heavy waxy or gummy residue is present, you may be dealing with a stain that will respond best to spot treatment with a drycleaning fluid. Since the appropriate removal method varies with the stain, start by using the least destructive stain removal methods first.

If the whole garment can be submerged, start by soaking the garment in cold water (as for protein stains). If not, use warm water and spot treatment technique. Next, use liquid detergent and lukewarm or hot water, rinse and let air dry (as for oil stains). If you suspect the stain is iron rust, treat with rust remover before bleach. If stain persists, use a pretreatment spray or solvent (as for combination stain) and all-fabric bleach. If the all-fabric bleach is ineffective on the stain and the garment is colourfast or white, finally try a dilute solution of liquid chlorine bleach.

Unique Treatment Methods

Chewing gum: Apply ice to harden gum. Crack or scrape off excess. Spray with pretreatment aerosol product. Rub with heavy-duty liquid detergent. Rinse with hot water. Repeat if necessary. Launder.

Deodorants: Apply liquid detergent, wash in warm water. Build-up of aluminum or zinc salts may be impossible to remove.

Fingernail polish: Do not use nail polish remover (or acetone) on acetate, triacetate, or modacrylic fabrics as they will dissolve. Take these fabrics to professional drycleaners and identify the stain. For other fabrics, use nail polish remover, acetone and spot treatment method.

Hog confinement odor: Wash clothes adding 1/4 to 1/2-cup household ammonia to wash load with heavy-duty detergent. Do not mix ammonia and bleach in same wash load. Toxic fumes are produced. Ammonia can be used on coloured fabrics, but occasionally its use will change the garment's colour.

Iodine: Iodine is quickly removed with sodium thiosulfate, which is sold in photo supply stores as "acid fixer." If the photo supply fixer solution contains other chemicals in addition to sodium thiosulfate, it should not be used. Iodine may also be removed by some commercial stain removers.

Lead pencil: Use art gum eraser to lift off excess; avoid hard rubbing. For delicate fabrics use spot treatment methods. For most durable, washable fabrics, spray with pretreatment aerosol product. Rub in heavy-duty liquid detergent. Rinse in warm water. Launder.

Mildew: Mildew is a growing organism that must have warmth, darkness, and moisture to survive. Mildew eats cellulosic fibers, causing permanent damage and weakening of fibers and fabrics. To remove mildew: Shake or brush item outdoors. Pretreat darkest stains with heavy-duty liquid detergent. Launder in hot water with a heavy-duty detergent. Bleach as safe for fabric.

Odor: Most odors are removed by laundering. For persistent odor problems, place calcium carbonate crystals, activated charcoal, or soda in an open container and store with clothes in closet or sprinkle soda directly on fabric and let stand; then shake or vacuum.

Paint-latex: Treat while wet. Soak in cold water; wash in cool water with heavy-duty detergent. After paint has dried 6 to 8 hours, removal is very difficult. Treat as combination stain. Wash in hot water, Rinse. Repeat treatment.

Paint-oil-based: Treat while wet. Use thinner recommended for paint. Use spot treatment technique and thinner on spots until paint is softened and can be flushed away in heavy-duty detergent wash. Usually turpentine or alcohol will work as solvents.

Perspiration: Apply liquid detergent or soak in warm water with presoak product 15 to 30 minutes. Launder.

Pesticide: If full-strength liquid concentrate spills on clothes, handle only with rubber gloves. Discard clothing immediately. Laundering does not remove concentrate to a safe level for reuse of clothing. Launder other pesticide-contaminated clothing separate from general family laundry. If visible staining from diluted spray of pesticide residues remains after laundering, rewash using hot water, heavy-duty detergent, and a full water level. Then line dry.

Rust: Rust stains cannot be removed in normal laundering. Use of chlorine bleach makes them permanent. Rust removers such as RoVer or Whink are effective and safe for most fabrics, but rust removers that contain hydrofluoric acid are extremely toxic, can burn the skin, and can damage the finish on appliances. A solution oxalic acid crystals in water will also remove rust stains,-but it is often difficult to obtain the crystals.

Lemon juice and salt are more readily available and are helpful sometimes, Sprinkle the salt on the stain, squeeze lemon juice on it and spread the garment in the sun to dry. A word of caution: Lemon juice can bleach some colours and many washable garments are not manufactured to be colourfast to sunlight.

Scorch: Excess heat on cellulosic (cotton, linen, ramie, rayon), wool, or synthetic fibers can cause permanent damage. If fabric is thick and fuzzy, brush to remove charring. Rub liquid detergent into scorched area. Launder. If stain remains, bleach using, all-fabric bleach. Fabric will be permanently weakened in scorched area. Synthetic blends that are melted or glazed cannot be fully restored.

Smoke, soot: Shake off excess soot outdoors. Launder in washing machine using heavy-duty phosphate-based detergent or heavy-duty liquid as recommended by manufacturer, one cup of water conditioner, and 1/2 cup of all-fabric bleach. Use water temperature appropriate for fabric. Air dry. Inspect for smoke odor. Repeat as necessary. Three or four washes may be needed for cottons and cotton blends.

Urine: Rinse in cold water and launder. For stains on mattresses: (1) sponge with cloth using detergent solution, (2) rinse with cloth using vinegar solution, (3) let air dry, and (4) if odor remains, sprinkle with soda or calcium carbonate; wait 1 day, then vacuum.

Water Spots: Launder. For drycleanable draperies, consult a professional cleaner. Water marks on drapes are water soluble and not removable by drycleaning solvents.

Common Remedies to Avoid

Dishwasher detergent: Although sometimes suggested for food stains, these detergents are intended for use in closed dishwashers with very hot water. They are so highly alkaline they can irritate your skin if you use them in stain removal. They also may fade colours or damage wool, silk, or nylon fibers.

Hair spray on ball-point ink: Certain hair sprays are effective on ballpoint stains, but they may deposit a gummy residue and perfume that then have to be removed along with the ink. Hair spray also may affect colour in some fabrics. Alcohol is a hair spray ingredient that is useful for removal of the oily part of the ball-point stain.

Ironing candle wax: Ironing candle wax between blotting paper will only drive the stain deeper into the fabric. This process is widely used, but it's not recommended because it will make any colour from the dye of the candle more permanently set and the wax more inaccessible for the detergent or solvent to reach to carry the stain away.

Milk on washable ink: This doesn't remove the ink and gives you an additional protein stain.

Salt to make dyes colourfast: Today's dyes cannot be increased in colourfastness by soaking in salt water. If bleeding of a particular dye in cotton, rayon, or ramie fabric is decreased with a salt water soak, the effect will not be permanent, When the fabric is wet again, unless there is salt in the solution, the dye will be free to leave the fabric. Salt cannot affect colourfastness of synthetic fiber fabrics or their blends because they are dyed with dyes that have chemical structures not affected by salt.

Shampoo: Clear gel-like shampoos are sometimes suggested for stain removal. While they are usually not harmful to fabrics and may work on light oil stains, laundry detergents are just as effective and less expensive to use. Additionally, coloured, opaque; or milky-looking shampoos may contain ingredients that will stain fabrics or foam so much that they are difficult to rinse out.

White vinegar: Vinegar (acetic acid) may weaken cotton, rayon, acetate, triacetate, or silk fibers and may cause colour change. If used as a stain removal agent, test on a hidden seam allowance for colourfastness. Vinegar will not help remove or set creases in today's synthetic or permanent press fabrics, although this is a common belief.

Preventing Staining Problems

Greasy-looking fabric softener splotches: Use of fabric softener sheets in the dryer can deposit softener unevenly, causing greasy-looking splotchy stains on silk-like polyester and blends of cotton/polyester broadcloth. This problem is especially noticeable on medium-coloured fabrics such as khaki and medium blue. Avoid this problem and control static by using a fabric softener that is added to the final rinse.

Odd coloured or rusty looking stains on collars, sheets and pillow cases, bedspreads, towels, or wash cloths: These stains are often caused by the benzoil peroxide used in cosmetic products (including acne medicine). This chemical acts as a bleach, is very insoluble and hard to rinse off the body. It can permanently change colours of some dyes. The damage cannot be remedied, So it should be prevented. When products containing this chemical must be used, white collars and household textiles may be a good choice.

Stiff, coarse textures and/or dull colours in freshly laundered fabrics: Nonphosphate granular detergents can combine with hard water to leave behind a residue that can cause fabrics to become stiff and feel harsh. Avoid the problem by using a phosphate-based detergent, a heavy-duty liquid detergent or a nonprecipitating water conditioner with the nonphosphate granular detergent. Soaking stiffened clothing in a solution of white vinegar and water (1 cup vinegar per gallon of water) may help restore them, however you should first test clothing for colourfastness to vinegar on a hidden seam allowance. Another way to restore this clothing is to treat as for yellow, gray, or general discoloration.

White powdery streaks on dark clothes: Powdery streaks on dark clothes are probably caused by undissolved detergent being incompletely rinsed out. Some nonphosphate detergents can deposit mineral hardness residue that shows as streaks. Avoid this problem by changing detergents or by adding detergent to the wash water first, then adding clothes and starting washer. Usually a repeat rinse and spin cycle with clear water will remove these streaks.

White streaks on blue jeans: White streaks on blue jeans are probably not caused by undissolved detergent. Blue jeans are often dyed with indigo dye, which is a fugitive dye that bleeds in a water solution. As the washer spins, the edges where the fabric is folded get more abrasion and rougher treatment, causing the colour to escape. Turning jeans wrong side out before laundering will reduce these white streaks and give more even fading. To avoid the natural fading that accompanies use of indigo, look for polyester/cotton jeans that are labelled colourfast. They will retain their dark blue.

Yellowing, graying, or general discoloration: This condition occurs when insufficient detergent issused for proper cleaning, wash water temperature is too low (especially for oil stains), too much detergent is used and insufficiently rinsed out, synthetics are washed with a light-duty detergent in cold water, or colour is transferred from other non-colourfast items in the wash.

To refurbish clothing with this discoloration, wash in a permanent press cycle with hot wash water, a cool-down rinse, and a cup of water conditioner instead of detergent. If discoloration persists, repeat this procedure or wash again using the correct amount of detergent, an all- fabric bleach, or diluted liquid chlorine bleach if safe for fabric.

The treatment of last resort for white items is treatment with a commercial colour remover. This reducing bleach must be used very carefully, as it will easily fade colours in any fabric it touches. If the yellow colour is on silk, wool, or spandex it may be a result of fiber alteration due to improper use of chlorine bleach and is not removable.

Treatment for Individual Stains

Acids: You must act quickly because strong acids (like battery acid) can damage fibers quickly. Splash with water immediately, then sprinkle the stain with baking soda, rub in, and allow to stand a few minutes until bubbling stops. Rinse well in warm water. Alternatively, hold the dampened stain over an open bottle of household ammonia so that the fumes can neutralize the acid. Rinse well.

Adhesive Tape: Sponge or soak the dry fabric stain with a suitable laundry pre-soak (spot stain remover) or in a grease solvent or kerosene. Kerosene will make the cloth oily, so if used, must be followed by washing in warm soapy water.

Alcohol: Whisky, vermouth, etc.: Always treat these as soon as possible. Often stains are almost colourless at first, but turn brown on standing, washing and ironing. Fresh stains can be removed by sponging several times with warm water. If there is any mark left, pour glycerine on the dampened stain, rub lightly between the hands and leave for half an hour. Rinse in warm water.

Stubborn stains may be sponged with equal quantities of denatured alcohol (or wood alcohol) and ammonia (test on colours first) or laundry pre-soak (spot stain remover). Rinse well in warm water. If any stain is left on white material, a laundry bleach may be used, if appropriate. Choose and use your bleach according to instructions given earlier.

Alkali and Strong bases: Alkali, such as caustic soda, strong ammonia, or alkali cuticle remover, may destroy colour and rot material. Rinse at once in equal quantities of vinegar and water. Rinse well in warm water. If colour has been affected this cannot be corrected.

Ball-Point Ink: If you are sure it is Ball-point (not roller ball) ink, then first, saturate material with an alcohol-based hair spray (this seems to be a very popular method). The alcohol content in the hair spray will break up the ink. Be sure to place an absorbent paper towel or rag under the stain to catch the excess. You then need to blot the stain with a rag. Repeat the process until the stain is removed, then launder as usual. A word of caution before trying this method: some fabrics may be damaged by the hair spray solution. If in doubt, test on an inconspicuous area first, or consult with a professional dry cleaner.

Baby Oil: Rub some dishwashing liquid into the stain, leave for 10-15 minutes, then wash in hot water using your normal laundry detergent. If any stain remains, repeat the process.

Bleach: Flood immediately with lots of cold water. For chlorine bleach, add 1 Tbsp. vinegar in each cup of water. If the colour has been removed by the bleach, it cannot readily be restored, but try holding in fumes from an open bottle of ammonia.

Blood: If still fresh, sponge with cool salted water (1 spoon per cup water) and rinse with clear water. For set blood stains, one of the best recommendations is the use of a commercial meat tenderizer (these are found in the spice section of your supermarket). Meat tenderizer breaks down the proteins in the fibrin strings that form when blood clots, allowing the stain to be released. Other suggestions are:

— Try an enzyme presoak

— Soak in a diaper wash/sanitizer that contains sodium percarbonate (follow label instructions)

— Try dilute hydrogen peroxide (1 part : 9 parts water). Rinse well. Be Careful, strong solutions of hydrogen peroxide can bleach fabrics.

— Sponge with a lukewarm 10% solution of Oxalic Acid for a few minutes, then rinse well. You can get this from the hardware store paint department or a pharmacy.

— Sponge with dilute ammonia (1 spoon per cup). Rinse well.

For thick or unwashable articles, e.g. mattresses, carpets, etc., sponge lightly with one of the above solutions. If the stains are still fresh, and the police have not yet arrived, sprinkle with meat tenderizer or pepsin powder (from your pharmacy), or spread with a thick paste of raw laundry starch and water, leave to dry, then brush off. Wipe with damp cloth an repeat if necessary.

Bluing (laundry bluing): Rinse fresh stains in cold water. Soak any more difficult stains in a solution 1 spoon of vinegar in a quart of warm water. Wash as usual.

Butter & Animal fat Stains: Wash in warm sudsy water if a washable fabric. If not, sponge dry fabric with a grease solvent, e.g. laundry pre-soak (spot stain remover) or dry cleaning fluid.

On upholstery and carpets, use an absorbent powder treatment (cornstarch is worth a try), followed by a shampoo with liquid detergent, such as a Carpet/Rug Shampoo, a good quality laundry liquid or Quilt/Wool Wash. Avoid wetting backing of carpet or fabric, or discoloration occurs.

Do not use petroleum solvents, or dry cleaning fluid on carpets or fabrics with rubberized backing. On wallpaper, scrape off as much as possible, then use warm iron and absorbent paper. Treat remaining stain with paste of cornstarch and a dry cleaning fluid. Allow to dry, brush off, and repeat if necessary.

Candle Wax: Scrape off most of the wax. This can be facilitated by placing the fabric in the freezer and making the wax brittle.

For the remaining wax, place the stained surface down on a clean white rag and spray with WD-40 (a light oil available at hardware stores), let stand a few minutes, turn fabric over and spray the other side. Apply liquid dishwashing detergent and work into the stained area, moving the rag as it absorbs the stain.

Wash in hot water with laundry detergent and bleach (if appropriate) for about 15 minutes (use heavy soiled setting if there is no minute timer on your machine) and rinse in warm water. Drip dry and check for residual stain.

In the case of coloured wax there may still be a colour stain. Sponge with a liquid made by adding a half cup of denatured alcohol to a half cup of water.

Carbon Paper & black soot: On washable fabrics heavy suds of soap and water are usually successful. Otherwise, sponge over a pad with denatured alcohol, followed with a cold water sponge.

Chewing Gum: Scrape or peel away as much as possible first. Rubbing the stain with ice will harden the gum and make this easier, especially on rugs and other heavy materials. Then follow the procedure under Candle Wax, above. If the material is washable, sponge with kerosene and wash in hot soapy water. For unwashable articles, use dry cleaning fluid. Several applications may be necessary.

Chocolate: First scrape off as much as possible with a dull knife. Scrub washable articles with an old toothbrush and hot soapy water. If a brown spot remains, soak in a solution of a diaper wash/sanitizer container sodium percarbonate followed by a good rinse in warm water.

For unwashable materials, sponge with dry cleaning fluid. Allow to dry. Repeat as necessary with a clean rag underneath. If a stain remains, sponge with equal quantities of denatured alcohol and household ammonia (test on colours first). Follow with a warm water rinse. A spray-on dry cleaner may be used.

Coffee & Tea: Remove fresh stains from cotton and linen materials by first rinsing in warm water then pouring boiling water from a height of 2 - 3 feet onto the stain. Follow by washing in hot soapy water. If a trace remains, bleach white garments in the sun, or with a diaper wash/ sanitizer container sodium percarbonate. Tea stains on cottons and linens can also be removed by soaking in borax and water (1 Tbsp. borax per cup of warm water).

Stains on wool and silk or any fabric may be sponged with lukewarm water, then apply glycerine, rubbing lightly between the hands. Let stand for half an hour. Rinse with warm water. If a grease spot remains from cream, sponge with dry cleaning fluid.

Crayons: Place the stained surface down on a clean white cotton rag, spray with WD-40 (a light oil available at hardware stores), let stand a few minutes, turn fabric over and spray the other side. Apply liquid dishwashing detergent and work into the stained area, moving the rag as it absorbs the stain. Wash in hot water with laundry detergent and bleach (if appropriate) for about 15 minutes (use heavy soiled setting if there is no minute timer on your machine) and rinse in warm water.

Kids throw a crayon into the dryer? Clean the inside drum of your dryer to remove any remaining wax residue. Spray a soft cloth with WD-40, and wipe the drum. Run a load of dry rags through a drying cycle to ensure that your drum is clean. Jump to Crayola's Stain Removal Tips for helpful hints on removing other art material stains from clothes, walls and other tough spots.

Deodorant Stains: Sponge stain thoroughly with a laundry pre-soak or spot stain remover and warm water. Rinse. If some stain remains in whites, use a chlorinated laundry bleach or a diaper wash/sanitizer container sodium percarbonate. Antiperspirants may cause fabric damage and colour damage in some dyes. Colour can sometimes be restored by sponging with ammonia. Dilute ammonia with an equal volume of water for use on wool or silk. Rinse well.

Dyes & Colour runs: Flood immediately with lots of water. These are difficult to remove and no one treatment is successful in all cases.

Washing and sun bleaching will gradually bring results in some cases. Equal parts of denatured alcohol and ammonia may also succeed. White fabrics may be bleached. Use a chlorinated laundry bleach or a diaper wash/sanitizer container sodium percarbonate for linens and untreated cottons, hydrogen peroxide for silk, wool and delicate fabrics.

Egg: Scrape away as much as possible. Sponge with lukewarm water immediately. Never use hot water, as heat sets the albumin. If this does not succeed, spread the stain with a paste of cream of tartar and water, adding a crushed aspirin to the paste. Leave for 20—30 minutes. Rinse well in warm water. OR use a diaper wash/sanitizer container sodium percarbonate.

Fruit & Berry stains: Fresh stains are easy to remove, but once dry, they are very obstinate. Treat immediately with cool water and follow up, if necessary, by soaking in a chlorinated laundry bleach or a diaper wash/sanitizer container sodium percarbonate. White cottons and linens may be stretched over a basin and boiling water poured through from a height. Any remaining stain may be removed with chlorinated laundry bleach.

Coloured fabrics or washable silk, etc., may be soaked in a diaper wash/sanitizer container sodium percarbonate or a warm borax solution (1 Tbsp. per cup of water), or covered with a paste of cream of tartar and warm water. Leave half and hour or until stain goes, then rinse well.

For persistent stains apply equal quantities of denatured alcohol and ammonia. Rinse well after treatment. This method is safe for all fabrics, except triacetate. Dilute mixture with an equal quantity of water for fabrics with fugitive dyes. Old stains may be softened in glycerine before treatment. Damp stain, apply glycerine, leave 1 - 2 hours, then add a few drops of vinegar, leave 5 - 10 minutes and rinse well.

Gasoline: Blot out as much as possible with a clean white rag. Place stain on a clean, white cotton rag. Spray with WD-40, and rub from the top with another clean rag. Flip over and spray stain from other side. Treat the edges of the WD-40 circle the same way to remove as much migrated material as possible. Soak in an enzyme pre-soak and then launder as usual. Drip dry and evaluate before putting in dryer. For dry clean only materials, take to the dry cleaners as soon as possible.

Glues, Gums & Cellulose Adhesives: Soaking in cool water will remove water-soluble glues, e.g. Elmer's, and most wood glue. For waterproof glues, use denatured alcohol, MEK or amyl acetate (test before using on synthetic fabrics). Artificial Fingernail glue can bc removed used acetone (test on an inconspicuous area first). Acetone evaporates quickly, so hold a wad of absorbent paper or soft cloth against the glue, and soak the acetate through from the other side. (The glue soaks on to the wad of absorbent)

Grass Stains: Soak in a solution of a chlorinated laundry bleach or a diaper wash/sanitizer container sodium percarbonate. OR sponge with methylated spirits (wood alcohol). Remove this with warm water and where possible wash the article using Laundry powder or Liquid.

Milk & Ice Cream: For washable materials, first sponge with lukewarm water, then wash as usual. If the material is not washable, sponge with dry cleaning fluid then with cold water.

Ink: Because INKS differ in composition it is impossible to find removers that are equally effective for all types of ink spots. The following is a range of suggestions from which you can choose. Dry the stained area. Mix together 3 parts dishwashing liquid with 1 part of denatured alcohol. Soak the stained area in this solution for 10-15 minutes. After the soak time, rinse in water as hot as is suitable for the fabric, then wash as usual. Drip dry and evaluate. This treatment may require repeating.

OTHER TREATMENTS

Ballpoint Pen Ink: First, saturate material with an alcohol-based hair spray (this seems to be a very popular method). The alcohol content in the hair spray will break up the ink. Be sure to place an absorbent paper towel or rag under the stain to catch the excess. You then need to blot the stain with a rag. Repeat the process until the stain is removed, then launder as usual. A word of caution before trying this method: some fabrics may be damaged by the hair spray solution. If in doubt, test on an inconspicuous area first, or consult with a professional dry cleaner.

Water Based Inks (roller ball, felt tip): Try an all-purpose cleaner like '409' instead of hair spray. Be sure to place an absorbent paper towel or rag under the stain to catch the excess. You then need to blot the stain with a rag. Repeat the process until the stain is removed, then launder as usual.

These suggestions are also suitable for dried writing ink, ball point pen, or marking ink. Soak the stain in "sour" milk - this is an old fashioned, but effective method. Fresh milk also works, but sour milk is faster to make sour milk, set a cup outside for several hours. Sponge or dip the stain in equal quantities of methylated spirits (wood alcohol) and household ammonia (test on coloured fabrics first). Rinse in warm water. Rinse again in warm water containing a little ammonia, then finally in fresh water. Sponge with denatured alcohol. If not effective, try dry cleaning fluid.

Iodine, Methiolate: Very fresh stains can often be removed by normal washing or by moistening the stain with water and placing in the sun. If not successful, apply a solution of 1 tsp. sodium thiosulphate, (from chemist) in 1 cup warm water. Rinse well.

Lipstick & Makeup: e.g. eyeshadow, mascara, etc.—washing with your usual laundry product may remove these stains. Pre treat the dry fabric stain with a laundry pre-soak (spot stain remover). On an unwashable fabric, try a discreet dry cleaners. If stains are stubborn, sponge with equal quantities of denatured alcohol and household ammonia. (Test on coloured fabrics first). If colour fades, reduce ammonia by half and test again. Rinse in warm water, or wash if possible.

Medicines: Try to find out from doctor or pharmacist what the medicine contains, as this will aid in selecting the correct treatment: e.g. iron tonics—treat as for iron rust: medicines containing alcohol, rinse with denatured alcohol, etc.

Mildew: Treat as soon as discovered, before the mould has time to weaken the cloth. Slight, fresh stains can often be removed by washing with your usual laundry product and drying in the sun. Otherwise, try these methods in turn, proceeding carefully with coloured articles:

Chlorinated laundry bleaches may be used for white untreated cottons and linens, 2 tablespoons per gallon should do it. Rinse thoroughly before washing. Vinegar added to the final rinse will help remove any traces of smell remaining from the bleach.

Oil & Grease

Mud: Allow to dry, then brush or scrape off. Any remaining stain may be removed by washing or sponging with your usual laundry powder, or if this is greasy dirt, pre-treat dry fabric with a laundry pre-soak (spot stain remover) or use a dry cleaning fluid.

Mustard: Scrape any excess mustard from the fabric, ensuring you don't spread the stain any further. Dry the mustard-stained area. Mix together 3 parts dishwash liquid with 1 part of denatured alcohol. Soak the stained area in this solution for 10-15 minutes.

Nail Polish: Apply acetone, MEK or nail polish remover, but take care with synthetics, as these may dissolve some type of rayons. Wash or sponge with your usual laundry product after treatment. Remove any remaining colour with a bleach, using a chlorinated laundry bleach for white cottons and linens. A diaper wash/sanitizer container sodium percarbonate for colours, and hydrogen peroxide for wool and silks.

Oils, light: sewing machine, cooking oil, baby oil etc. Rub some dishwashing liquid into the stain, leave for 10-15 minutes, then wash in hot water using your normal laundry detergent. If any stain remains, repeat the process.

Scrape away as much as possible with a spoon. Place stain on a clean, white cotton rag. Spray with WD-40 (available at hardware stores), and rub from the top with another clean rag. Flip over and spray stain from other side. Continue to flip, spray, rub and move to a clean area of the rag until the stain is removed. Treat the edges of the WD-40 circle the same way to remove as much migrated material as possible. Soak in an enzyme pre-soak and then launder as usual. Drip dry and evaluate before putting in dryer.

Another method is to use a mechanics hand cleaner (available at auto parts stores), gently rubbing it into the stain with a tooth brush. Follow with an enzyme pre-soak and then launder as usual. Drip dry and evaluate before putting in dryer.

For dry clean materials, treat with WD-40 as above, and take to the dry cleaners. Tell them you were greasing your 1956 Pickup.

Ointment: Treat as a grease stain.

Paint: Paint varies greatly in composition and it is not possible to give one treatment for all types. As a guide, use the solvent suggested on the paint can label for thinning paint and cleaning brushes. Treat promptly, as set stains are very difficult to remove. If paint has dried, soften with glycerine before applying treatment.

For oil paint, enamels and alkyd type paints, scrape off as much as possible and spray with WD-40 or soak in turpentine, or kerosene. Then wash in usual way.

Latex and water-base paints will wash out easily with soapy water when fresh. Remove any remaining colour stain with denatured alcohol. Once dry, these paints are virtually impossible to remove.

Pencil Marks: Try a soft eraser for unwashable garments. Use a quality laundry powder or liquid on lead pencil marks, but never for Permanent marker. If not successful, follow instructions for Permanent Marker.

For coloured pencils, place the stained surface on clean rag, spray with WD-40, let stand a few minutes, turn fabric over and spray the other side. Apply liquid dishwashing detergent and work into the stained area, replacing towelling as it absorbs the stain. Wash in hot water with laundry detergent and bleach for about 12 minutes (use heavy soiled setting if there is no minute timer on your machine) and rinse in warm water.

Perfume stains: Wet area, apply glycerine and rinse out well, or sponge with equal parts of full-strength hydrogen peroxide (on whites) and water. If the colour has already been removed from the fabric by the alcohol in the perfume, it may be helpful to add a few drops of denatured alcohol to cheesecloth pad and sponge fabric lightly, working towards the centre of the stain, thus distributing remaining colour evenly.

Permanent markers: Do not use water as this spreads the stain. Sponge over a pad of soft cloth, using equal quantities of denatured alcohol) and household ammonia (test coloured fabrics first). Should the colours run, try denatured alcohol) alone. Rinse or sponge with warm water.

Perspiration Stains: New perspiration stains are normally acid and may be removed by washing. If the fabric dye is affected, hold the mark in fumes from an open ammonia bottle to try to restore the colour. Older perspiration stains turn alkaline and sponging with 1 Tbsp. vinegar in a half cup of water will often restore the colour. This treatment also helps to remove perspiration odors.

To remove perspiration stains from unwashable garments or for any stubborn marks, apply a paste of 1 Tbsp. cream of tartar, 3 crushed aspirins and a cup of warm water. Leave for 20 minutes. Rinse well in warm water. Repeat if necessary. Follow this with vinegar and water to restore the colour if necessary.

Rust (Special thanks to Lois Lane's dentist for these tips): Any of the methods given below are safe for white fabrics, but test on coloured fabrics before use.

— *Lemon Juice*: suitable for light stains on delicate fabrics. Spread stain over a bowl of boiling water and sprinkle with lemon juice. After a few minutes, rinse well and repeat if necessary.

— *Lemon Juice and Salt*: Sprinkle stain with salt, rub with lemon juice and place in sunlight. Keep moist with lemon juice till stain goes. Rinse well.

— *Cream of Tartar*: (a powder, available in your grocery store spice section) for extensive staining, boil in a solution of 3 tsp. cream of tartar per cup of water. Rinse well OR if less extensive, dampen stain, spread with cream of tartar, hold in steam from boiling kettle. Rinse immediately stain goes. Do not use on fabrics that cannot be washed in hot water.

Scorch Marks: Scorch marks on cellulosic fibers (cotton, linen and tencel) are different from true stains in that the actual fibers are damaged. Severe marks on any fabric, and scorch marks on wool and silk can seldom be restored. Brushing with fine emery paper may improve a scorched woollen surface. Very light scorch marks can often be removed by immediate washing with your usual laundry product, followed by a day in the sun. Alternatively, sponge with 1 Tbsp. borax in 1 cup of warm water.

Light scorch marks on white materials can be bleached with hydrogen peroxide. Dampen a rag of white cotton cloth with hydrogen peroxide and lay it covering the mark. Cover with a clean dry cloth, then press with a medium warm iron. If the peroxide soaks through the top cloth, move to a dry position. Repeat the treatment until the stain is removed. Rinse well in warm water.

Light scorch marks on any fabric (test colours first) may be treated by sponging with diluted hydrogen peroxide to which a few drops of ammonia have been added. Rinse well in warm water.

Shoe Polish: Sponge with a laundry pre-soak (spot stain remover) or with dry cleaning fluid.

Silly Putty: Scrape off the excess with a spoon or blunt knife, then spray the surface to be cleaned with WD-40 and wipe clean with a soft cloth. If any stain remains, saturate a cotton ball with rubbing alcohol, blot the stain and rinse. Wipe any remaining residue with a damp sponge or cloth moistened with liquid dishwashing detergent.

Skunk Smell: If you or your clothing or hair gets sprayed by a skunk, wash with carbolic soap to remove the skunk oil or alternatingly in tomato juice and then vinegar. One of our alert readers with a dog that got sprayed regularly has suggested a Massengill Douche powder solution works better than anything else she tried. Might be worth a try.

Commercial smell removers are available like "Skunk-off" aerosol, or "Nil-Odor" available through your Vet Clinic. Clothes may have to be discarded, although in less severe cases they may be salvaged by repeatedly washing in vinegar water and hanging outside for about a month. Launder clothes in cool water as hot water causes oil to break down and stink up the laundry room.

Soft Drinks: Pre-treat with a laundry pre-soak prior to washing with a your usual laundry detergent in the usual way. Alternative treatment: sponge with equal quantities of denatured alcohol) and water. Old or obstinate stains may be softened in glycerine before treatment as above.

Soot & Smoke: First treat with an absorbent powder like cornstarch, then wash. For unwashable articles sponge with dry cleaning fluid or other grease solvent, followed by airing to remove smell of smoke.

For carpets, mix solvent to a paste with cornstarch, talcum or french chalk. Apply thickly - leave to dry, then brush or vacuum off. Repeat if necessary. Never use solvents on rubber backed carpeting.

Soy Sauce: Dry the soya sauce-stained area. Mix together 3 parts dishwash liquid with 1 part denatured alcohol. Soak the stained area in this solution for 10-15 minutes. After the soak time, rinse in water as hot as is suitable for the fabric, then wash as usual, but preferably with a Laundry Liquid. This treatment may require repeating.

Tar & Asphalt: Scrape away as much as possible with a spoon or dull knife. Place stain on an old cotton rag. Spray with WD-40 (available at hardware stores), and rub from the top with another clean rag. Flip over and spray stain from other side. Continue to rub and move to a clean area of the rag until the stain is removed. Magic! Treat the edges of the WD-40 circle the same way to remove as much migrated material as possible. Soak in an enzyme pre-soak and then launder as usual. Drip dry and evaluate before putting in dryer. For dry clean materials, treat with WD-40 as above, and take to the dry cleaners.

Tarnish Stains (from Brass or silver): Metallic stains from belts, jewellery, etc., sometimes stain clothes. Sponge with vinegar, lemon juice or 10% solution acetic acid (check synthetics first).

Tobacco Stains: For stubborn tobacco stains, first try pouring glycerine over the stain. Rub lightly between the hands, or pre-treat the dry fabric with a laundry pre-soak (spot stain remover), leave for half an hour then wash in the usual way. If this is not successful, use sodium thiosulphate as directed for iodine stains.

Tomato Stains: Sponge thoroughly with cold water first. Pour glycerine over, rub lightly between the hands and leave for half an hour. Or, pre-treat the dry fabric with a laundry pre-soak (spot stain remover), leave for half an hour then wash in the usual way. Rinse in warm water. Remove any remaining stain with a chlorinated laundry bleach or a diaper wash/sanitizer container sodium percarbonate, as directed.

Whiteout (Liquid Paper) (Liquid Correction Fluid): Purchase some Spray & Wipe from your supermarket, and use concentrated on the stain. Most Spray & Wipe formula's contain a solvent which will dissolve the liquid paper. OR Try a little xylene, or toluene on the stain, with some good absorbent paper or old cloth behind it. Then use some dishwash liquid or a good quality laundry liquid to wash out the solvent. Always test an inconspicuous piece of material before proceeding.

If a stain cannot be identified, treat with cool water first, then sponge with a good quality laundry liquid solution. Rinse well and if stain persists try equal quantities of denatured alcohol and ammonia, testing first to note effect on colour and fabric. If colour is affected, omit ammonia. As a last resort, try a mild bleach, e.g. A diaper wash/sanitizer container sodium percarbonate.

Urine: These stains differ in composition from pets to people, so that the same method may not be successful in all cases. Normal urine is usually slightly acidic, so first soak or sponge in a solution of a diaper wash/sanitizer container sodium percarbonate or sponge with a solution of 1 Tbsp. household ammonia in a half cup of warm water. Rinse well.

If this is not successful, try equal quantities of vinegar and warm water in case the stain is alkaline. Rinse well in warm water. For stubborn stains, sponge with diluted hydrogen peroxide, then wash or sponge—rinse with clear warm water. Old stains may destroy the colour of the cloth and nothing can be done to restore it in this case.

Vomit : Scrape away as much as possible. Sponge stains with warm water containing a little ammonia. If extensive, dampen and sprinkle with pepsin powder (from the pharmacy), leave half an hour, then rinse off. OR soak washable articles in a diaper wash/sanitizer container sodium percarbonate. Commercial carpet cleaners may work.

Water Spots: Some silks (organza, notably), rayons and wools are spotted by water. To remove such spots, hold in the steam from a rapily boiling kettle. It is wise to cover the spout with muslin first to prevent any droplets of water reaching the fabric. Allow the fabric to become damp, but not wet. Shake and press while still slightly damp, rubbing, if possible, with a piece of the same or a similar material, or with fingernail or spoon.

Water stains on carpets become brown because of impurities from backing or underfelt. Mop up spills, wipe with cool water, cover with pad of blotting paper, tissues or absorbent cloth. Weight down with books, etc., and dry quickly with the aid of fan heaters, vacuum exhaust, etc. This causes stain to wick through to absorbent material.

Red Wine: Immediately pour club soda or White Wine on the affected area and soak up. Then wash in cold water and ammonia.

White Wine: Club soda rinse, then wash in cold water and ammonia. If unsuccessful, follow other treatments under Alcoholic Beverages, above.

Wood SAP: Scrape with a spoon and sponge with a mix of 1 part Turpentine and 4 parts dishwashing liquid. Leave for 20 minutes and then wash with your usual laundry detergent as water as hot as the fabric will allow. You may have to repeat this process.

5

TABLE CLOTHS AND NAPKINS

Tabletop components like-flatware, plates, or glassware—table linens are one-dimensional. The foodservice term for table linens is napery. In addition to providing colour, napery also offers the greatest "comfort level" of any tabletop item. Tablecloths and napkins are the only items that don't have hard surfaces, and they should feel good, as well as look good.

One manufacturer of tablecloths and napkins suggests that five basic table colours-white, red, hunter green, royal blue, and rose petal pink-can be used by any restaurant to create festive moods year-round for any holiday theme. Some common examples are listed below.

— *Red, White, and Blue*: Any patriotic holiday

— *Red and Green*: Christmas and New Year's Day

— *Red, White, and Green*: Cinco de Mayo or other Hispanic festival days; Italian holidays or events

— *Red or Pink and White*: Valentine's Day

— *Pink and White*: Weddings, Mother's Day

— *Green*: St. Patrick's Day, Thanksgiving

No matter what colour or fabric is used, the linens, won't have the desired effect if they are not spotlessly clean. Clean napery fulfills the restaurant's promise of a safe, clean place to eat. Besides the basic tablecloth and napkin, there are placemats and table runners. Runners are lengths of fabric that are placed down the centre of a table (often over the tablecloth) to introduce a complementary print or accent colour to the tabletop. They are sometimes known as decomats.

Some restaurateurs use two tablecloths on each table, putting on a larger cloth first, then covering it with a second, smaller tablecloth. The smaller cloth, called a top or overlay, is changed more often than the larger one. In busy restaurants, using tops makes busing the table easier and less noisy, while enabling you to introduce an accent colour with the top. Often, though, tops and the cloths beneath them are both the same colour.

As a foodservice operator, you will have so many choices of materials and colours that it helps to have some basic knowledge about the fabrics from which napery is made. Even if you decide to rent instead of buy your linens, you'll get better service from the rental company (and you'll be able to tell your staff how to care for the items) if you know something about how they are made. Textile fibers may be natural or synthetic, but they all have a base that is either cellulose (plant) or protean (animal/ insect). Examples of cellulose-based fibers are cotton, flax, and hemp, which begin their life cycle as plants. Examples of protein-based fibers are silk, wool, or other cloths that begin as part of an animal or insect.

The two types of fiber react differently to heat, moisture, dye, and other variables that govern their suitability for foodservice use. Cotton begins as the puffy, fibrous material that surrounds the boll (or seedpod) of the cotton plant. It is thin and twists easily, so many small cotton fibers are woven together to make long, strong strands that can then be woven into cloth.

Cotton is relatively inexpensive. As a fabric, it is durable and absorbent; in fact, it actually becomes stronger when it gets wet. It is also flexible and does not attract static electricity, and both qualities make it an attractive choice for draping tables. On the negative side, cotton shrinks and stains rather easily. Fortunately, modern technology allows us to treat today's cotton fabric so it resists both these tendencies. The fancy term for making cloth shrink-proof is to make it dimensionally stable.

Linen is a bast fiber, meaning it comes from the inner portion of a plant stem. This particular plant is flax, and it yields long fibers (up to 3 feet in length), as well as short ones. The finest linen comes from the longest fibers. Linen, like cotton, absorbs moisture well and is stronger wet than dry. It is two to three times stronger than cotton and good-quality linen does not shed lint like cotton often does.

However, linen does not retain its strength under the rigours of laundering. Bleaches and harsh detergents are more likely to damage linens than cottons. Linen has a stiff, crisp feeling because the fibers used to make it are not very flexible. It wrinkles and creases easily, but it is also nonstatic and holds dye well. There are other cellulose-based fibers, such as ramie, jute, and hemp, but they are not widely used as table coverings. Nor are protein-based fabrics, such as wool (from animals) or silk (from insects). They just wouldn't hold up to the heavy use they'd receive in a restaurant. However, there are several synthetic fibers in common use in foodservice settings. These include rayon, acetate, nylon, polyester, and combinations thereof.

Rayon is a cellulose-based fabric, made from bits of wood, cotton, and other cellulose products. Acetate begins its life as the same basic cellulose mixture, but different chemicals are added to each mixture in the manufacturing process. Both rayon and acetate are flammable unless specifically fireproofed. Both fabrics are low in cost. Second only to cotton, rayon is one of the world's most popular fabrics. It dyes well and can be made shrink resistant; it also absorbs moisture and can be laundered or dry-cleaned with equally good results.

However, rayon lacks strength and resiliency and is easily attacked by acids and/or alkalies. Acetates also launder well and can be bleached without problems. Acetate fabrics have soft, luxurious textures and good draping qualities. They don't hold dyes well, though, and, unless specially treated, they build up static electricity. They must be ironed at low temperatures, too, because they'll glaze, stick, or even melt under an iron that's 300 degrees Fahrenheit or hotter.

Nylon is a nitrogen compound, a mixture of several nitrogen-based chemicals. Nylon has the disadvantage of not absorbing moisture well, and it tends to build up static electricity unless it is treated with an antistatic coating. Although nylon is strong and durable, it will yellow with repeated washings. Nylon must also be washed, dried, and pressed at moderate heat settings.

Polyester is a current favourite of both manufacturers and foodservice professionals. It's a synthetic concoction of glycerin and a variety of acids and goes by a number of brand names: Dacron, Vycron, and so on. Polyester is strong, easy to dye, easy to wash, dries quickly, resists wrinkles, and doesn't shrink or fade. Some people don't like the "slick" feeling of polyester, which tends to slide off the customer's lap and onto the floor. From a budget standpoint, however, polyester lasts much longer than cotton. An odd characteristic of polyester is that it's not very water absorbent, but it soaks up oil quickly.

Polyester fabrics must be specially treated to prevent stains from typical foodservice sources such as ketchup, iced tea, and lipstick. In their endless quest for customer satisfaction, manufacturers are always tinkering with their synthetic fabrics, trying to come up with combinations that work better than cloths made from individual fiber types.

To date, the most popular amalgam is 50 percent cotton, 50 percent polyester, commonly known as the 50/50 blend.

Restaurateurs favour blends because they are such faithful reproductions of the textures of all-natural fabrics, but they don't stain as easily. The best of both worlds? Well, yes and no. The 50/50 blend is certainly stronger than cotton, more colourfast, and less likely to shrink; it also absorbs spills as well as cotton. However, its polyester content means it absorbs oily spills, too, which makes for some nasty stains if they're not treated promptly. Heat, bleach, and mildew can wreak just as much havoc on a 50/50 blend as on 100 percent cotton. Experts agree the 50/50 blend offers a lot of convenience, but, overall, you end up with a product that wears and looks more like polyester than like cotton.

A study done for the table linen industry about a decade ago indicated a couple of statistics that are probably timeless: 93 percent of all diners notice whether a restaurant's napkins are cloth or paper, and 78 percent prefer cloth, saying it "upgrades" their expectations of the dining experience. Indeed, the types and styles of napery you use will convey the degree of sophistication of your dining establishment. So consider the following factors as you look at samples and talk with salespeople.

Fashion: In some ways, table fashions mirror clothing fashions. Although cotton is a popular choice, today's fast-paced lifestyle often requires the durability and convenience of synthetics. Always examine potential linens with other tabletop components. At this writing, placemats and table runners are "hot" accessories, and it's no longer chic to simply roll up a napkin into a tube when you could make it into a more interesting shape, or stuff it attractively into an empty glass to add height to a table setting.

Also consider the overall impact of the colours on the entire room, not just on a single table. In choice of colour, remember that tablecloths in a warm, fall hue may look dramatically out of place next spring; or that the Southwestern print tops you're ready to order won't fit if you're not serving that type of food six months from now.

Budget: If your tables are showing wear and tear, you can buy new tables or cover the old ones. Yes, purchasing tablecloths is less expensive in the short run. However, from then on, you must factor in the costs of cleaning, repair, and replacement. When it comes to napkins, an Illinois Restaurant Association survey found the cost difference between using cloth and paper is only 2 to 3 cents more per meal for cloth, since diners tend to use two to three paper napkins, but only one cloth napkin.

Environment: Many foodservice operations use fabric napery simply because their customers think using throwaway paper products is wasteful. Others spurn polyester because it is not biodegradable. Environmental issues such as recycling and waste disposal are important to customers and should be to you in your decision making.

Tactile Sensations: Multiple surveys indicate that restaurant patrons simply prefer natural fibers for napkins. They say they "feel better" than synthetics. The tactile quality of a fabric is called its hand in the linen industry. However, consider carefully what sensation you wish to convey. High-dollar, formal restaurants want the feeling of crisply starched linen, while a more casual place can choose a softer material. Some restaurants use padded tables, which gives a nice, soft feeling but can cause stemware to topple more easily Padded tables cannot be used without tablecloths.

Lifestyle: Although casual dining seems relaxed, do not confuse it with a lack of sophistication. The use of nice linens can add just the right touch of class to a menu of upscale burgers and microbrewed beers. Diners don't expect mediocrity when they dine out, and your tabletops should exceed their expectations. On the other hand, decide whether your target clientele will "accept" a tablecloth. In their minds, it may mean they "have to" dress up when they don't really want to.

Menu: Family restaurants or barbecue restaurants will be harder on their linens overall. Is it worth it to buy table linens if you'll always be stain treating them?

Technology: Keep up with the market, long after you've made your initial purchases. This is a very competitive field and manufacturers are continually improving the quality of tabletop fabrics. Ask to see new samples now and then.

Napery Needs

How many tablecloths? How many napkins? These are not easy decisions. Too much inventory ties up capital; too little necessitates frequent washing, which means excessive wear, which means more expense replacing napery! To avoid this vicious cycle, you've got to do some homework. There are several different options for obtaining and laundering your table linens:

— Rent them from a reliable rental service.

— Purchase the fabric yourself, have it cut and hemmed to the sizes you need, and hire a professional laundry to wash and iron it on a regular basis for a fixed price per pound. There should be regularly scheduled pick-up and delivery times. In a written contract, spell out the consequences if these are not met or if the laundry loses or damages any of your napery. Buy your own and wash it yourself. A linen inventory requires some ongoing maintenance and a budget to replenish it as items wear out. However, by laundering it yourself, the experts suggest you can save 50 percent over what it costs to rent table linens. If there is space available, perhaps the most economical alternative is to have your own on-premise laundry room.

— Buy your own and hire your mom to do the wash.

Questions of quality, size, and colour can only be answered after you have made a battery of other decisions about your restaurant's concept, design, price range, and menu. If nothing else, you can't pick out tablecloths unless you know the sizes and shapes of your tables. If yours is a completely casual or fast-food venue, you'll probably stick with paper products. If it's a franchise operation, the size, style, colour, and imprinting of napkins or placemats may be dictated by your parent company.

For other types of restaurants, however, cloth should at least be considered. When you buy your own linens, most napkins and tablecloths can be cut to order. However, they do shrink slightly when laundered for the first time, depending of course on fabric type. What does it matter if your guest puts a 16-inch or a 20-inch square of cloth on his or her lap? If you're going to use certain types of classy-looking napkin folds or if you want to give the appearance of luxury (like an oversized towel in a nice hotel), you'll choose a bigger napkin.

For tablecloths, choose the correct size by adding 8 to 12 inches to the size of your tabletop. Twelve inches is the usual amount of space between the table and the seat of the chair. The amount of tablecloth that hangs over the side of the table is called the drop. The drop should not interfere with the guest's comfort getting into and out of a chair or booth, but it should be long enough to completely cover all ends of the table and to drape attractively.

Napkin Sizes,Before are After Laundering

Cut Size (inches)	Laundered Size (inches)
13 x 18	11 x 16

16 x 16	14 x 14
16 x 23	14 x 21
18 x 18	16 x 16
21 x 21	19 x 19
22 x 22	20 x 20
24 x 24	22 x 22

For banquet tables, one option that may be less expensive than buying finished tablecloths is to buy fabrics in standard widths (54-, 64-, 72-, or 90-inch) and have them cut and hemmed to fit 6- to 8-foot tables. Even more economical, purchase your tables in small, standard sizes. You can always accommodate larger parties by moving tables together and covering them with smaller tablecloths, eliminating the need for larger ones.

A reliable guideline is the "rule of three:" For every cloth on a table, there should be a clean cloth in inventory awaiting use and a third one in the laundry. To determine your own target number, begin by multiplying your total number of tables by your turnover rate.

Renting Linens

Working with a linen-rental company is another opportunity to build a good business relationship. You can rent more than table linens from these firms. Most also offer kitchen towels, aprons, and uniforms; and it's nice to have a supplier for special occasions when you need table skirting and different colours or types of linens that you wouldn't otherwise have in inventory.

A big part of shopping for this service is checking the company's references. Ask other customers about the kind of service they provide. Be wary of the linen-rental company that proposes charging you a flat fee by the week for a maximum number of linens. What this really means is that, each and every week, you're charged to keep the same 400 tablecloths in stock, even if you only used 150 of them.

Always arrange to pay based on what you actually use, for a fixed price per use. In the contract, a price should be quoted per napkin and per tablecloth, depending on the sizes of napkins and/or tablecloths. Some colours or fabric blends may be more expensive than others. All of these variables should be listed in writing, along with:

— Specific quantities to be delivered
— Times and days for pick-up of soiled linens and delivery of fresh ones
— Your recourse, if anything goes wrong

It's tempting to accept incoming orders without the hassle of counting them, since they are neatly bundled for storage, but they should be counted if possible. Be sure to note if you're short a few napkins, and set aside any that are stained or damaged, and then ask for credit for these pieces. The linen company contract usually includes a replacement charge for each item that is damaged. Monitor these "replacement charges" carefully. It's not out of line to ask to keep the damaged items. After all, you're paying for them outright when you pay that replacement charge.

Also ask the rental service what happens (charges or penalties) if linens disappear, because pilfering is an unfortunate reality of the restaurant business. When interviewing both linen-rental and laundry-service companies, look for added value. Will they come in periodically and help train your employees about linen care, or offer stain treatment guidelines and products? Again, these are long-term partnerships. Make sure you are getting that "partnership feeling" from these important suppliers.

If you're going to buy or rent hundreds of napkins, you might as well have some fun with them. The way napkins are folded says a lot about the attention paid to detail in your dining room. Most are quite simple, for the elegant effect they can have. Try different folds on your tabletop to see which ones look the best.

Paper Napkins

There's nothing wrong with using paper products. Many family restaurants bedeck their tables with white butcher paper and furnish crayons so the kids can draw on it. Even more eateries use paper napkins. Those who prefer paper say it is:

— Easy to use and discard
— Easy to store and takes up less space than cloth
— Safe and sanitary
— An additional way to advertise when imprinted with name or logo
— Less expensive than cloth

Paper napkins come in a variety of sizes. It seems the most difficult thing to control, especially in a self-service or takeout setting such as a cafeteria or fast-food restaurant, is that customers use so many napkins. The tendency is always to take more than they need. Some restaurants use paper napkins for breakfast and lunch service, then switch to linens for a more upscale mood at dinner. The casual, theme restaurants were the first to eliminate the tablecloth altogether.

The marketing implication is clear: to position themselves somewhere between fast-food and white-tablecloth dining. A decorative table can be attractive with no cover at all, and the cleanup is quicker and easier, too. Also, the table itself can be used as a marketing tool, to mirror the theme of the eatery. The trend begins with the idea that, like the walls of your dining area, table surfaces can also be decorated to embellish the atmosphere.

Colourful tiles, postcards, sports memorabilia just about any- thing whimsical may be embedded into the tabletop itself, which is then sealed to prevent stains and water damage. The tabletop itself may be made of ceramic tile, although this is unadvisable because it can crack or chip with use. The restaurant's walls feature custom-designed tiles, but using tile on tabletops was not practical.

Instead, tabletops and countertops were surfaced with DuPont Corian, with random patterns of tiny, multicoloured epoxy triangles embedded in a solid colour. It's a fun look, like confetti scattered across these surfaces, and helps set the stylish, casual mood for these upscale pizzerias. The use of glass tops over tables is another alternative. A tablecloth may still be used, but the glass fits over it exactly, minimizing spills and stains. Cleanup of the table is certainly easier, but take into account the increased noise level as dishes and flatware clank onto the hard surface. If you choose glass-topped tables, buy heavy plate glass with polished edges.

Sharp corners snag on fabrics and are more likely to chip. An interesting advantage of the glass-topped table is that it allows you to experiment with fabrics not necessarily used as tablecloths; the rich colours and patterns of upholstery fabrics, for instance, which are dry-cleaned about three times a year instead of being laundered. Because the glass covers the table surface, your cloth choices are much wider. Yet another easy-maintenance alternative is the vinyl table covering.

A good, commercial-grade vinyl has a soft, cushioned backing to muffle noise, and wipes clean with a damp cloth. It comes in several thicknesses, from 4-gauge (the thinnest) to 10-gauge (the heaviest). Vinyl can be used for upholstering booths and chairs, too, and is appropriate for fast-food, casual, and outdoor dining establishments. If your vinyl covers will be used on outdoor umbrella tables, be sure you order them with a strong stitch on the umbrella hole. If not, you will soon be reordering, because just a few windstorms will pull at the cloth enough to tear it around the opening.

Like fabrics, vinyls can be purchased as yard goods and customised to fit your table sizes. There are also laminated table coverings-choose from hundreds of existing designs, or select any fabric, purchase it by the roll, and have it laminated, cut, and sewn to fit your tables. Laminated cloth looks more upscale and "linen-like" than vinyl. The initial cost of laminating can be daunting-$6 or $7 per yard, in addition to the cost of the fabric itself-but remember, it will last for several years, at least. Laminated cloth does not have the cushioned backing like vinyl, but you can order inexpensive, nonslip padding to use beneath the cloth.

Care and Cleaning

Unfortunately, the people who work for you may actually work against you in your crusade for great-looking table linens. This is the real world, and napery is likely to be used as everything from a dishrag to a potholder as it makes its way from tabletop to laundry and back again.

Research by the American Hotel-Motel Association indicates tablecloths and napkins are washed an average of 100 times before they are discarded as ragouts, the informal term for making them into rags. However, they would last longer if they were not abused by foodservice staffers. Linen replacement costs the typical restaurant from 13 to 25 percent of its laundry budget, so it is worth your while to convince employees that the sole purpose of a napkin is to place on the dining table. Don't wipe with it, use it to grab hot pans or dishes, or wrap the flatware in it when tables are being cleared. There should be a training process for handling linens in your business. It should include:

— Educating employees about the cost of linens and the importance of handling them correctly. A system for sorting soiled linens by item and colour into different hampers. This applies whether you do your own laundry or use a rental service.

— Procedures, supplies, and a specific place to pretreat stains before tossing items into the hampers.

— A place to put damaged linens that must be inspected and/or returned to the rental company. Some control of who has access to the linen supply to prevent theft, including a sign-out or check-out system for obtaining linens.

In addition to training of your wait staff and busers, there are other factors to consider in your choice of linens:

Colour Retension: You'll want some assurance from your salesperson that the colour will remain consistent, no matter how many times the item is washed. This is also known as being colourfast.

Soil/Stain Release: When properly laundered, all of the typical restaurant stains and odors should wash out easily. The now-famous Scotchguard process is advisable for many types of fabric. It coats the fibers to prevent even the toughest food stains, and enables you to wash the items successfully without heavy-duty laundry equipment.

Absorbency: No matter how crisply it is starched and ironed, the fabric should maintain its ability to soak up liquids.

Finish: The surface of a napkin should cling to a customer's lap without sliding off; permit fancy folds; and feel natural and somewhat soft, even when it's been starched. Remember, in the industry, the feel of a fabric is called its hand.

Minimal Shrinkage: After their initial shrinkage, both napkins and tablecloths should maintain their basic square shape. The latter should retain its ability to drape the table attractively.

Lack of Lint: Who wants to stand up from an important business lunch to find bits of white stuff all over that nice dark suit? Lower grades of fabric break down more easily in the wash process and produce more lint. Choose fabrics that won't shed.

An important part of the staff training process mentioned earlier is treatment of problem stains immediately after a meal, before they can "set." Some restaurants have a policy of putting a loose knot in a stained or soiled item (like a napkin), or in a separate plastic bag (like a tablecloth), to signal that it needs special attention. This also keeps it from staining other items when placed in the same laundry bin or hamper. Your laundry service may recommend a professional-strength stain remover that is safe for the kinds of fabrics you're using.

There are also some tried-and-true "restaurant remedies:"

— Berry and other fruit stains, or red wine spills, can be sprinkled with salt, or saturated with club soda, or both.

— Mildew or rust spots respond to repeated applications of a paste of lemon juice and salt. (Rinse completely before reapplying the paste.)

— Coffee or tea stains and iron scorch marks can be lifted out of white linens by soaking them in a solution of one part borax to six parts water.

— Similar coffee-type stains that have been sitting long enough to dry onto the fabric can disappear when rubbed gently with a mixture of glycerin and water.

Just remember that, if you're going to soak something to remove a stain, don't soak it for more than fifteen minutes. Any longer and you're just soaking the fabric in the dirty water. Your stain may have come out, but the whole napkin may look dingy from then on. If your restaurant has its own linens and laundry, give someone the responsibility of checking it periodically for wear and tear. Rips only get bigger in the wash, so they should be mended before laundering.

There's a whole list of laundry "dos" and "don'ts." Your linen supplier probably has suggestions, and so will the instructions that come with your commercial washers and dryers. Here are a few of the top tips from foodservice operators and commercial laundries with restaurant clients:

— Sort and wash colours separately four to five times before washing them with whites or other colours.

— The minimum wash temperature should be 140 degrees Fahrenheit, but no higher than 160 degrees Fahrenheit. Lower water temperature won't sufficiently clean; hotter water will fade fabrics faster.

— Set the machine for the proper water levels for your wash load.

— Use only detergents that are labelled correctly, use the right amounts, and add them at the right times.

— Avoid overloading the dryer. Load dryers to 60 percent of capacity when you will be tumble-drying without ironing afterwards; 80 percent of capacity when planning to iron the fabric.

— If your dryer has a cool-down cycle, use it. It's best to dry fabrics completely and gradually cool them to about 100 degrees Fahrenheit before they are removed from the dryer.

— All napery should be ironed while it's still damp. Especially if you're going to starch an item, pass up the dryer altogether and iron immediately after washing.

— Iron table linens at temperatures between 315 and 350 degrees Fahrenheit; lower isn't effective and higher will damage them.
— Over-starching linens will make them more fragile.

If you're not ironing them, remove them promptly and fold or drape immediately. Avoid mildew by storing clean tablecloths on coat hangers with plenty of air circulation, instead of folding and stacking them. Fine linen needs time to "rest" after being cleaned, to restore a bit of its natural softness. Newly washed, dried, and folded linens should be stored at least 24 hours before being returned to service.

Doing restaurant laundry is not as simple or mindless a process as you might assume. Another leading table linen manufacturer, Artex International, Inc., suggests you perform a few simple tests on samples of your selected fabric. By determining the right detergents and temperatures to use, you will get the maximum useful life out of your napkins and tablecloths. These tests include bleaching samples of the fabric, first with only a mild concentration of bleach, and then with a high bleach concentration, to see how the fabric reacts. This should help determine the amount of bleach to use.

Bleach does not technically remove stains; it simply oxidizes them to appear colourless. It should always be used sparingly, and with caution. You'll also want to check with the napery manufacturer to see which type of bleach is recommended, if any, depending on the type and colour of fabric: chlorine, sodium hypochlorite, or sodium peroxide. Other tests can indicate the fluidity of the fabric (how much a single wash can damage it); the re-deposition rate (how much dirt or lint is "redeposited" on fabric that is improperly washed-not enough detergent, overloading the machine, and so on); and the effects of temperature and water acidity or alkalinity.

An alkalinity check of your water is especially important, because this will affect how well the soap dissolves in the water and how thoroughly the fabrics can be rinsed. The pH level of the wash water should never be lower than 7. You can purchase heat-sensitive strips to measure the temperature of your wash water within 10 degrees, or simply stop the machine and use a thermometer. Water softeners and filters can help enormously with sediment build-up in appliance water lines, and also with rust-related stains.

Rust is dissolved iron in tiny particles that are difficult to filter out, and can make light-coloured fabrics look dull over time. In areas where rust is an ongoing problem, commercial laundries use a product known as a "sour" in the rinse water, to dislodge rust particles. Yet another type of laundry technology "zaps" linens clean without heat, detergents, or bleach. Hotels that have field-tested the system claim their laundry bills were cut by 60 percent.

On-premise Laundry

The most economical long-term method of handling linens is known as the on-premise laundry. It is used in high volume-hotels and motels, hospitals, and colleges-because they also wash bed linens. Athletic clubs and country clubs may have sufficient laundry volume, between dining linens and towels. In fact, any restaurant or catering facility that produces more than 500 soiled napkins and 100 soiled tablecloths per day is probably a candidate for an on-premise laundry. One benefit of doing it yourself is that you'll never get caught short on weekends or holidays. However, operations with lower counts should carefully weigh the costs of owning versus renting from a reliable linen supply firm.

In estimating your laundry volume, don't forget to include kitchen and bar towels, aprons, and uniforms, if applicable. The decision to install a laundry room is a big investment of money, as well as space. Once it's in place, it will cost a lot to run (electricity) and a lot to maintain (repairs). So weigh these factors carefully:

— Initial cost of the equipment

— Installation charges (plumbing, electrical)

— Utility costs (electricity, water)

— Ongoing supply costs (detergents, bleach, and the like)

— Repair and maintenance costs

— Cost of hiring or training someone to run and maintain the facility and troubleshoot when necessary

— Cost of purchasing all napery

— Costs to repair napery when necessary

The development of wrinkle-free (more accurately, "noniron") fabrics has prompted more foodservice managers, especially in casual establishments, to consider on-premise laundries. They can be run by less-skilled personnel, don't use as much hot water, and the linens themselves are less expensive than higher-maintenance cottons. If you decide to move in this direction, your three major considerations should be economy of operation; consistent quality of the finished linens; and selection of the right person to accomplish these goals.

Give careful thought to the location, size, and construction of a laundry room. Unlike the washer and dryer tucked neatly into a pantry or large closet at home, this laundry will need space for: worktables for receiving and sorting; the machines; an extraction area (moving items from washer to dryer, which, in very large operations, can be done mechanically); ironing and folding; linen storage, and checkout. The size of your laundry facility will be determined by your volume of business, number of seats, types of table covers, and more.

Napery Trouble Shooting Guide

Problem	Cause	Solution
Discoloration	Bleach on colours	Do not use bleach on colours.
	Residual dye	Prewash colours separately on first wash transfer to prevent residual dye transfer. Sort napery into recommended colour groupings for subsequent washings. Always wash whites separately.
	Soil redeposition	Reclaim napery with soil redeposition by using increased temperature and supplies. Prevent redeposition by adjusting the formula for soil level.
	Chemical reaction	Avoid chemical discoloration by thoroughly rinsing all chemicals out of the napery before drying or finishing.
	Yellowed whites	Chlorine bleach will not damage VISA* fabric, but residual bleach on white napery can cause yellowing if the chlorine is not neutralized before exposure to heat. Avoid yellowing by using an antichlor, in the second rinse after bleaching with chlorine.
	Incorrect ordering	Order napery colours by the four-digit code number or the distributor colour codes to avoid confusing similar colours.

	Glazing	Keep ironer chest temperatures under 350°F and use correct roll pressures to prevent glazing.
Waterproofing	Fabric softeners	Fabric softeners prevent VISA napery from absorbing liquids. Do not use fabric softeners on PISA napery.
	Tallow soap	Do not use tallow soaps on VISA napery. Instead, use built detergents and surfactants.
	Mildeweides cotton	To help minimize mildew growth on VISA napery, use only mildeweides that have no quaternary ammonium base.
	Washing with cotton	Wash PISA napery with other 100°h synthetic fabrics. Do not wash with cotton or palycotton blends.
	Soil redeposition	See Discoloration—Soil redeposition.
	PYAc buildup	Reclaim, then reformulate the starch ratio: four parts natural starch to one part PYAc.
Static	Overdrying	Reduce extraction or conditioning, and cover wet work to maintain 20-25°lo moisture retention in napery before ironing.
	Incorrect grounding	To effectively ground equipment, sink a 6′ steel rod in the ground and attach grounding straps. Also, use static bars on folders and conveyors.
	Friction	Eliminate friction from goods slipping on the belts by synchronizing the speeds of adjacent belts.

	Folders	Check folder adjustments and/or use more starch on napery.
	Low humidity	Low relative humidity can cause goods to stick due to static electricity. On particularly dry days, a humidifier may be needed.
Stains	Permanent: Bleach spots/cleaners carbon/metal heat set food/ cement	For all permanent stains, try reclaiming with more supplies and higher temperatures to reduce stain visibility. Napery with noticeable stains should be ragged, overdyed by a qualified dye house, or cut into smaller pieces.
	Removable: Blood	Use a warm water flush, then normal washing. Do not use hot water on protein soils.
	Fats/corn oil	Use solvated surfactants to boost salad dressing regular formula.
	Motor oil/grease	Use solvated surfactants to boost regular formula.
	Lipstick/candles wax	Use solvated surfactants and/or higher temperatures.
	Rust	Use an oxalic acid prewash or rust-removing sours.
	Mildew	Use chlorine bleach on whites. As a last resort, use 1% available chlorine bleach at 1-2 quarts/ CWT to remove mildew from coloured napery.

		This will cause some colour deterioration. A mildeweide with no quaternary ammonium base should be used to minimize mildew growth.
Ironing rejects	Dirty ironer	First, do a thorough downtime cleaning. Then follow up with regular cleaning and maintenance checks.
		Do not overwax the ironer to avoid wax buildup.
	Roll pressure	Do the paper test on the first ironer roll. Correct uneven or incorrect pressure.
	Side-to-side pressure	Check bearings, individual roll pressures, and the pillow blocks.
	Drafting	Check the circumference of each roll with adding machine tape to determine if there is appropriately increasing diameter from front to back. If not, replace the ironer padding.
	Incorrect feeding	Carefully instruct all personnel on correct feeding procedures.
	Cold chest	Maintain a minimum chest temperature of 310°F
	Warped chest	A warped chest must be replaced.
	Over- or undersoured napery	Adjust the amount of sour to maintain 5.5-6.5 pH.

	Ironer tapes	Be sure there are two ironer tapes per lane for napkins. Tapes should be around the ironer rolls and tension bars only, not around the finger roll.
	Residual chemicals	Rinse goods thoroughly, then sour to neutralize rinse water alkalinity. Also, thoroughly clean the ironer chests and roll pad covers to remove chemical buildup.
	Goods too wet	Increase extraction or conditioning if napery is too wet going into the ironer. Goods should feel damp at the recommended 20-25% moisture retention.
	Roll motion and covers	Correct rough roll motion and loose or rough roll covers. Also check for excess wear on covers, belts, and aprons.
	Static	See Static-Grounding.
	Glazing	Keep ironer temperature under 350°F and maintain 20-25% moisture in napery to avoid glazing.
Customers picks and snags	Rough shelves and table corners	Eliminate rough spots and protruding nails on shelves. Tape table corners.
	Personnel	Educate personnel on correct handling techniques.
Laundry picks	Burrs and sharp edges	Check for burrs and sharp edges on

and snags		machinery and handling equipment by using a wet VISA napkin. Do not use staples to fasten ironer tapes, and check for loose or broken wires on feed and exit apron connectors.
	Washing with tableware	Be sure all tableware and other foreign objects are removed before washing.
Starch/sizing	Too stiff: PVAc buildup or excessive starch	Reclaim with additional alkali and more heat. Then reformulate four parts natural starch to one part PVAc.
	Too limp: Water level	Use lowest available water level for optimum starch penetration. Actuat' level varies by washer.
	Sour	Starching results are best at pH levels between 5.5-6.5. Add sour at least two minutes before starch to allow even distribution.
	Temperature	Maintain bath temperatures between 90 and 100°F for starch.
	Supplies	Check with your Milliken Technical Services Representative for the recommended amounts and ratios of supplies for each type of starch or sizing material.
	Load size	Starch penetration is limited when the washer is overloaded. Use the following clean dry

		weight capacities as a guideline for load size: full drop: 90%, split pocket: 75%, Y pocket: 65%.
	Overdrying	Too much extraction or conditioning causes starch to be lost. Maintain 20-25% moisture retention in napery before ironing.
	Time	Allow at least eight minutes starch time for even penetration of starch.
	Inadequate cleaning	Reformulate washing process to ensure thorough cleaning of napery so starch can adhere to the fabric.
	Personnel	Carefully instruct all personnel on correct starching procedures to insure consistency from load to load.
Wrinkles	Thermal shock	Thermal shock wrinkles occur when napery is exposed to sudden changes in temperature. Avoid thermal shock by tempering cold water in the winter. Then reduce the water temperature in 15° increments to 100°F before extracting.
	Extraction	Reduce pressure, RPM, or time during extraction.
	Insufficient cool down	Cool to a temperature of 140°F or less before extracting or removing from washer or dryer.

	Hot spots on dryer	Be sure gas flame is not impinging on the dryer basket.
	Malfunction	Inspect all machinery and maintain on a regular schedule.
	Overloading	Washer capacity should not exceed 90% of clean dry weight for full drop machines, 75% for split pocket, and 65% for Y pocket. Tumbler loads should be 50%. Also, do not leave carts or slings overloaded for extended periods.
	Folder stacks	Reduce the size of napery stacks on the folder or increase airflow to cool the napery before stacking.
	Storage	Fold napery correctly before storing, and allow adequate storage space to prevent wrinkling.
Folder rejects	Settings	Check manufacturer's recommendations for correct settings.
	Slippage	Inspect and maintain gears, belts, and conveyors at the apron/conveyor junction. Also, try slowing down the conveyors or using more starch.
	Uneven folds	Adjust folder alignment to manufacturer's specifications and repair or replace worn belts.
	Belt angle	Reduce the incline if the conveyor belt angle is too sharp.

	Static	See Static—Grounding, and check the speeds of adjacent surfaces.
	Dirty folder	Clean each folder and folder belt with an air hose as needed.
	Personnel	Carefully instruct all personnel on correct feeding techniques and lane alignment.
Customer abuse	Excessive heat	Explain to the customer that excessive heat such as a hot grill will damage linens.
	Incorrect storage	Set up storage for both clean and soiled napery in a convenient place. Check to be sure correct procedures are being followed.
	Soil segregation	Advise the customer not to mix soiled napery with bleach rags or bar wipes.
	Incorrect usage	Napery should not be used as a grease rag or bar wipe. Offer the customer appropriate items for these applications. VISA is a registered trademark of Milliken and Company for fabrics.

*VISA is a registered trademark of Milliken and Company for fabrics

For example, let's examine the needs of a restaurant that soils 500 napkins and 100 tablecloths per day: Here, one washer-extractor and one dryer could be installed in an area as small as 120 square feet. But where would cleaning supplies be stored? Where would ironing be done, and clean linens be stored? You must make room for at least two worktables, as well as the machines themselves, and the best way to store tablecloths is on hangers in an area with good air circulation to prevent molding.

Soiled linens must also be stored somewhere until washing, and hampers should be out of sight of guests. Your laundry should be located near the receiving area at the back of the house, preferably on an outside wall of the building to provide venting for the dryers. Modern technology also allows for design of the equipment exit vents so that the hot air passes through a heat exchanger and is reclaimed. Some commercial dryers have heat reclaimers built in. A ground-floor location is ideal because, of course, laundry is heavy. The walls and floors of this area should be made of durable, moisture-resistant material, highly insulated to keep noise to a minimum.

You don't need windows in the laundry area, because wall space is better used for storage shelves and bins. However, in some cities they are required, so take care to place them where glare won't be a problem for employees. Place them high up on the walls, and use wireglass (sheet glass with wire netting embedded in it) to prevent breakage. Doors should be large enough to get the washers and dryers into the room in the first place, and to enter and exit easily with utility carts or baskets in tow. Windows in this set of swinging doors should provide a clear view to prevent accidents; bumper guards on the doors can be placed so the utility cart can be used to shove the door open without scratching or denting either door or cart.

Door thresholds should be flush with the floor so there are no bumps to clatter over. A 9- to 11-foot ceiling is recommended, and sound absorption is especially important. The floors should be level concrete slabs, capable of supporting the heavy cleaning machines. Have floor drains installed near the washer sites, and the floors sloped about 1/2 inch per foot toward the drains to facilitate runoff in case of water overflow or backup. Other than the areas directly around the drain, no part of the floor should be a low spot where water could pool.

Concrete is the most suitable floor material, but for employees' comfort and safety, it should be covered with mats made of nonskid rubber or other synthetic material wherever people will be walking or standing. These facilities require lots of utilities. You'll need hot water, cold water, steam vents, and gas and/or electricity, as well as large (6-inch) drains and 1-inch water lines. Preplanning is essential to accommodate all these requirements. Your appliances will probably require electrical outlets for both 115- and 220-volt use, and at least 100 psi of steam pressure.

Ceiling light fixtures should provide at least 40 to 50 foot-candles of illumination, and all fixtures should be vapour-proof so they're not affected by the humidity that is a natural byproduct of doing laundry. Both humidity and temperature can be controlled by exhausting the machines to the outside and installing exhaust fans within the room. Of all the utilities you'll juggle, water is among the most important.

Hard water is undesirable for an on-premise laundry. It contains mineral salts, which can mix with the alkaline cleaning chemicals to become a sticky mess known as soap curd. Soap curd looks just like it sounds; it sticks to fabric, making it so stiff and unsightly that it can cut its useful life by half. It may also discolour some fabrics. It is such a potential problem that both hot and cold water should be softened before use in a commercial laundry. Softening should be considered when the hardness of your incoming water supply is rated between 5 and 10 grains, or 171 parts per million of solids. Consult your local water department when making this decision.

Laundry Equipment

The appliances you buy should be able to handle both lightly and heavily soiled laundry. Shop for washers and dryers with a variety of cycles and temperatures to launder the wide range of fabrics you will be using. Make sure the interiors are large enough to accommodate your bulkiest items and largest loads. Look for large door openings (for easier loading and unloading) at convenient heights (to prevent back strain).

Today's commercial washers and dryers are highly computerised, with microprocessor controls instead of electrical contacts and wiring. They're built to save energy, and they can often be preprogrammed. You might consider purchasing two smaller washing machines instead of a single, big one. It will take less time to accumulate enough laundry for a full load, and you'll always have a backup in case one machine needs to be serviced.

You can handle smaller loads or odd lots more efficiently and/or wash two types of items simultaneously. Again, the average home-use washer is simply not built for the wear and tear of restaurant use. The commercial washer even does its job differently than a home machine. Instead of a central agitator, a commercial machine launders by lifting and tumbling the linens in its internal cavity, which is called a cylinder. If the cylinder is small, the lifting and tumbling action is limited-not good for getting things really clean. Often, a commercial washing machine is installed by being bolted to the floor. This keeps it firmly in place.

But the latest commercial laundry technology is a floating suspension washer, also called a soft-mount washer. It does not have to be bolted down, since it does not "vibrate" during the spin cycles like a regular washer. It was created primarily for hotel use, so that washers on guest floors didn't create annoying noise and vibration when they were running, but it's a useful option if space is tight and vibration or unbalanced loads are problems. Floating suspension washers also spin laundry much faster than their regular commercial counterparts, running at higher revolutions per minute (rpms).

The faster a machine's spin cycle, the less moisture in the items that emerge from the washer. That means less drying and ironing time. Another way to accomplish this is with an extractor. As its name suggests, this machine extracts moisture from wet fabrics by spinning them around under high-speed centrifugal force-so fast that the wet fabrics weigh only 11/2 times what they would if they were completely dry. Commercial washer-extractor combinations are available, which require less space and eliminate the step of having to remove wet laundry from the washer and place it in the extractor.

A washer-extractor with a 35-pound capacity will take about 25 minutes to complete both wash and extract cycles. Some of these machines also have a cool-down cycle, during which cold water is slowly injected into the wash to prevent non-iron fabrics from wrinkling. The capacities of these machines vary from the 35-pound model (about the same size as a home washer) up to the 700-pound model for large hotels and hospitals.

When you see the volume of linens most restaurants use, it should become clear that there isn't a soul who would consider pressing it by hand. That's why there are commercial ironers and folders. Most napery can be sent directly from the extractor to the ironer. The ironer gives napkins and tablecloths a crisp, finished look. Often, even no-iron fabrics are sent through the ironer to improve their appearance. The ironer/folder step is sometimes called finishing.

The ironer may run on gas, steam, or electricity, but the principle is the same: It is a continuous-feed machine with rollers. Linens are sent separately through the row of rollers, emerging warm and neatly pressed on the other side. For tablecloths and napkins, the standard finishing temperature is about 338 degrees Fahrenheit, but this temperature can (and should) be adjusted when fabric instructions call for it.

If some types of linens are ironed too hot, they develop a shiny, unattractive glaze. An automatic folder takes over when pressing is finished. The linens are fed directly from one machine to the next. The folder acts as an extra pair of hands, holding the laundry, then blasting it with air to make sharp creases. Modern folders have computer chips in them, to calculate the specific points at which folds should be made and time the air blasts accordingly.

Ironers are identified based on how many pounds they can handle per hour; the smallest models range from 40 to 100 pounds per hour. Be sure you purchase an ironer that is large enough to handle your widest tablecloth, and consider a dual-finish machine, which irons the fabric on both sides at once. Not all your laundry will be extracted, ironed, and folded, so you'll also need at least one dryer. Commercial dryers are also known as tumblers.

The tumbler should have about 25 percent more capacity than your washer and/or extractor; that is, pair a 35-pound washer with a 50-pond dryer; or 100-pound washer with a 125-pound dryer. In fact, you should probably have more dryers than you have washers, so multiple loads can be drying simultaneously Dryers should be located close to washers and extractors, to minimise employees' having to lug loads across the room.

Today's commercial dryers have more efficient heating elements and new lint removal methods. Some feature fire suppression systems, in case of overheating. Just toss in the kitchen towels and come back when they're dry? Finally, worktables with casters are the most convenient spots for folding the items that don't receive automatic folder treatment. These tables can be moved as needed. You'll also need plenty of baskets and hampers, each holding a minimum of 12 to 16 bushels. There should also be ample cupboard and bin space to store the full complement of detergents, stain removers, bleaches, and fabric softeners you will need.

6

USE OF CARPETS AND PADS

Carpet is a flooring material which is comfortable to walk on, can be cleaned, and offers a luxurious appearance. The term was also used for table and wall coverings, as carpets were not commonly used on the floor in European interiors until the 18th century. The hand-knotted pile carpet probably originated in Mongolia or Turkestan between the 4th and 2nd millennium BC. Carpet-making was introduced to Spain in 10th century by the Moors.

The Crusades brought Turkish carpets to all of Europe, where they were primarily hung on walls or used on tables. Only with the opening of trade routes in the 17th century were significant numbers of Persian rugs introduced to Western Europe. Some use the words carpet and rug interchangeably. Historically, however, some have distinguished between carpet and rug based on size (the former being larger) or use (carpets on floors, rugs on beds or on the hearth).

For the sake of clarity, some textile scholars also differentiate between carpets and carpeting. In this usage, the latter are wall-to-wall and are often woven or tufted as "roll goods", most often in 12 foot widths but sometimes in up to 15 foot widths. In the real estate and home improvement industries a distinction is made between carpet (or carpeting) and rug. The former indicates a covering that is affixed to a floor and the latter a floor covering that is loose-laid, most often for decorative purposes.

Types of Carpet

There are many different carpets on the market with beautiful colours, surface textures, and varying qualities. One of the most important aspects of carpet quality is the density of the carpet. Density refers to the number of yarn tufts per square inch of carpet. The denser the carpet, the longer the carpet will look new. A good way to check carpet density is to fold the back of the carpet onto itself, which allows you to see how tightly packed the yarns are at the fold. If you can see a lot of the backing, the carpet may not be a good buy.

You can compare two pieces of carpet by folding each carpet piece onto itself and comparing how closely the yarns are packed together (Figure 1, Density). Sometimes carpet density is confused with pile height and face weight. Just because a carpet has a long pile height or high number for face weight does not mean the carpet is dense or wears well.

Figure 1. Density

A long pile height gives carpet a luxurious appearance. However, the longer the pile height, the greater the tendency of the carpet to mat, especially in high traffic areas.

If you want a deep pile carpet, select an extra dense carpet. Face weight is a measure of the total amount of yarn on the front of the carpet. Increasing the pile height and the density increases the face weight. The face weight alone, however, does not determine quality because weight can be increased with just pile height. Two carpets could be the same face weight and yet be quite different in quality and performance.

Swatches of Machine-made Carpet

A flatweave carpet is created by interlocking warp (vertical) and weft (horizontal) threads. Types of oriental flatwoven carpet include kilim, soumak, plain weave, and tapestry weave. Types of European flatwoven carpets include Venetian, Dutch, damask, list, haircloth, and ingrain (aka double cloth, two-ply, triple cloth, or three-ply). A hooked rug is a simple type of rug handmade by pulling strips of cloth such as wool or cotton through the meshes of a sturdy fabric such as burlap. This type of rug is now generally made as a handicraft.

On a knotted pile carpet (formally, a supplementary weft cut-loop pile carpet), the structural weft threads alternate with a supplementary weft that rises from the surface of the weave at a perpendicular angle. This supplementary weft is attached to the warp by one of three knot types to form the pile or nap of the carpet. In the late 19th century moquette came to mean wall-to-wall carpeting.

However, its historical usage refers to supplementary warp cut or uncut loop pile made on a draw loom (aka Velour d'Utrecht, Brussels, Wilton, bouclé, and Frisé). These textiles have a low pile and are thinner than hand knotted pile carpets. This form of carpeting, made as early as the 16th century, is constructed on a mechanized loom like velvet: the supplementary warps loop under the weft and are attached without forming a knot. Because of the loom structure only five colours can be used to create the design.

Moquette is woven in relatively narrow panels (usually 27" or 36"). Larger works are composed of several stripes sewn together. Moquette carpets have been used on floors, tables, as furniture upholstery, and wall coverings. Production was improved with the application of the Jacquard mechanism in 1812 in France and c. 1825 in England. The addition of steam power in the mid-19th century further improved manufacturing capabilities.

Swatches of Berber carpet

Unlike woven carpets, embroidery carpets are not formed on a loom. Their pattern is established by the application of stitches to a cloth (often linen) base. The tent stitch and the cross stitch are two of the most common. Embroidered carpets were traditionally made by royal and aristocratic women in the home, however, there has also been some commercial manufactory since the 16th century. That century saw a rise in production due to the introduction of steel needles (earlier needles were made of bone) and improvement in linen weaving.

Mary Stewart Queen of Scots is known to have been an avid embroiderer. 16th century designs usually involve scrolling vines and regional flowers (for example, the Bradford carpet). They often incorporate animal heraldry and the coat of arms of the maker. Production continued through the 19th century. Victorian embroidered carpet compositions include highly illusionistic, 3-dimensional flowers. Patterns for tiled (composed of a series of squares) carpets, called Berlin wool work, were introduced in Germany in 1804. They became extremely popular in England in the 1830s.

Several less expensive, machine-made carpet types were invented 19th-century in Great Britain. Tapestry brussels and tapestry velvet production began in 1832. These techniques minimised waste by printing different colours on the same thread eliminating the need to use different spools. In 1839 James Templeton developed a chenille technique. His carpets were called Patent Axminster in reference to the more expensive, hand-knotted Axminster rugs. Steam power was applied to these looms in 1884. Although production continued until the mid-20th century, chenille carpeting declined after the invention of Spool Axminster (1878) and Gripper Axminster (1890). These types were developed from the American Halcyon Skinner's 1860s invention called the "nipper".

Knotted Pile Carpet

Both flat and pile carpets are woven on a loom. Both vertical and horizontal looms have been used in the production of European and Oriental carpets. The warp threads are set up on the frame of the loom before weaving begins. A number of weavers may work together on the same carpet. A row of knots is completed and cut. The knots are secured with (usually 1 to 4) rows of weft. There are three main types of knot: symmetrical (also called: Turkish or Ghiordes), asymmetrical (also called: Persian or Senna), and single warp (also called: Spanish).

Contemporary centers of oriental carpet production are: Pakistan, India, Turkey, Northern Africa, the Caucasus, Iran, Nepal, Turkmenistan, Tibet, and Pirot. The importance of carpets in the culture of Turkmenistan is such that the national flag features a vertical red stripe near the hoist side, containing five carpet guls (designs used in producing rugs). When buying a modern carpet from Asia, many consumers wish to ensure that it has not been made using child labour. A labelling scheme in throughout Europe and North America has been therefore created called Rugmark. Importers pay for the labels which pays for monitoring in the centres of production and for education of previously exploited children.

Early Carpets

Pazyryk carpet

The hand-knotted pile carpet probably originated in Mongolia or Turkestan between the 4th and 2nd millennium BC. The earliest surviving pile carpet in the world is called the "Pazyryk Carpet". It is usually dated to the 5th century BC. It was excavated by Sergei Ivanovich Rudenko in 1949 from a Siberian burial ground where it had been preserved in ice in the valley of Pazyryk.

The origin of this carpet is debated. It has been proposed to be a product of either the Iranian Scythians or the Persian Achaemenids. This carpet is 200 x 183 cm (6'6" x 6'0") and has 360,000 knots/m^2. The earliest group of surviving knotted pile carpets were produced under Seljuk rule, in the first half of the 13th century, on the Anatolian peninsula. The eighteen extant works are often referred to as the Konya Carpets. The central field of these large carpets is an overall geometric repeat pattern. The borders are ornamented with a large-scale, stylized, angular calligraphy called Kufic, pseudo-Kufic, or Kufesque.

Oriental carpets

Oriental carpets began to appear in Europe after the Crusades in the 11th century. Until the mid-18th century they were mostly used on walls and tables. Except in royal or ecclesiastical settings they were considered too precious to cover the floor. Starting in the 13th century Oriental carpets begin to appear in paintings (notably from Italy, Flanders, England, France, and the Netherlands). Carpets of Indo-Persian design were introduced to Europe via the Dutch, British, and French East India Companies of the 17th and 18th century.

Spanish carpets

Although isolated instances of carpet production pre-date the Muslim invasion of Spain, the Hispano-Moresque examples are the earliest significant body of European-made carpets. Documentary evidence shows production beginning in Spain as early as the 10th century AD. The earliest extant Spanish carpet, the so-called Synagogue carpet, is a unique survival dated to the 14th century. The earliest group of Hispano-Moresque carpets, Admiral carpets (also know as armorial carpets), has an all-over geometric, repeat pattern punctuated by blazons of noble, Christian Spanish families.

The variety of this design was analysed most thoroughly by May Beattie. Many of the 15th-century, Spanish carpets rely heavily on designs originally developed on the Anatolian Peninsula. Carpet production continued after the Reconquest of Spain and eventual expulsion of the Muslim population in the 15th century. 16th-century Renaissance Spanish carpet design is a derivative of silk textile design. Two of the most popular motifs are wreaths and pomegranates.

French carpets

In 1608 Henry IV initiated the French production of "Turkish style" carpets under the direction of Pierre Dupont. This production was soon moved to the Savonnerie factory in Chaillot just west of Paris. The earliest, well-known group produced by the Savonnerie, then under the direction of Simon Lourdet, are the so-called Louis XIII carpets. This is a misnomer, however, as they were produced in the early years of Louis XIV's reign (circa 1743-1761). They are densely ornamented with flowers, sometimes in vases or baskets.

The designs are based on Netherlandish and Flemish textiles and paintings. The most famous Savonnerie carpets are those made for the Grande Galerie and Galerie d'Apollon in the Louvre between c. 1665-1685. These 105 masterpieces, made under the artistic direction of Charles Le Brun, were never installed as Louis XIV moved to Versailles in 1678. Their design combines rich acanthus leaves, architectural-style framing, and mythological scenes (inspired by Cesare Ripa's Iconologie) with emblems of Louis XIV's royal power.

Pierre-Josse Perrot is the most well-known of the mid-18th-century carpet designers. His many surviving works and drawings display graceful rococo s-scrolls, central rosettes, shells, acanthus leaves, and floral swags. The Savonnerie manufactory was moved to the Gobelins in Paris in 1826. The Beauvais manufactory, better known for their tapestry, made knotted pile carpets from 1780 to 1792. Carpet production in small, privately owned workshops in the town of Aubusson began in 1743. Carpets produced in France employ the symmetrical knot.

English carpets

Knotted pile carpet weaving technology probably came to England in the early 16th century with Flemish Calvinists fleeing religious persecution. Because many of these weavers settled in South-eastern England in Norwich the 14 extant 16th and 17th century carpets are sometimes referred to as "Norwich carpets." These works are either adaptations of Anatolian or Indo-Persian designs or employ Elizabethan-Jacobean scrolling vines and blossoms. All but one are dated or bear a coat of arms.

Like the French, English weavers used the symmetrical knot. There are documented and surviving examples of carpets from three 18th-century manufactories: Exeter (1756-1761, owned by Claude Passavant, 3 extant carpets), Moorfields (1752-1806, owned by Thomas Moore, 5 extant carpets), and Axminster (1755-1835, owned by Thomas Whitty, numerous extant carpets). Exeter and Moorfields were both staffed with renegade weavers from the French Savonnerie and, therefore, employ the weaving structure of that factory and Perrot-inspired designs.

Neoclassical designer Robert Adam supplied designs for both Moorfields and Axminster carpets based on Roman floor mosaics and coffered ceilings. Some of the most well-known rugs of his design were made for Syon House, Osterley Park House, Harewood House, Saltram House, and Newby Hall. Six of Axminster carpets are known as the "Lansdowne" group. These have a tripartite design with reeded circles and baskets of flowers in the central panel flanked by diamond lozenges in the side panels.

Axminster Rococo designs often have a brown ground and include birds copied from popular, contemporary engravings. Carpets will forever be associated with the town of Kidderminster in Worcestshire, United Kingdom. This was the heart of the UK carpet industry throughout the industrial revolution. Even now, a large percentage of the 55,000 population town still seek employment in this industry.

Scandinavian carpets

The traditional Scandinvian carpet is the rya, made from hand-knotted wool. Dating from the 15th century, the first ryas were coarse, long-piled, heavy covers used by fishermen instead of furs. The rugs became lighter and more ornamental. By the 19th century they were often splendid festive tapestries. Now, the rya is a painting in textile, with individual artists identifiable by the colours, patterns and techniques.

Modern Carpeting

Carpeting is an attached floor covering made of a heavy, thick fabric, usually woven or felted, often wool, but also cotton, hemp, straw, or a synthetic counterpart. It is typically knotted or glued to a base weave. It is made in breadths to be cut, seamed with a Seaming Iron and seam tape, but formerly it was sewed together, and affixed to a floor over a cushion (pad) using nails, tack strips, or adhesives, thus distinguishing it from a rug or mat which are loose-laid floor coverings.

Carpeting which covers an entire room area is loosely referred to as 'wall-to-wall,' but carpet can be installed over any portion thereof with use of appropriate transition moldings where the carpet meets other types of floor coverings. Carpeting is more than just a single item; it is, in fact, a system comprised of the carpet itself, the cushion, and a method of installation.

'Carpet tiles' are squares of carpet, typically 0.5m square, that can be used to cover a floor. They are usually only used in commercial settings and often are not affixed to a floor in order to allow access to the subfloor (in an office environment, for example) or to allow rearrangement in order to spread wear. Modern carpeting is often attached to the floor (or stairways) of a building and, when considered permanently attached, would be part of the real property which includes the building.

When shopping for carpet, do not think that just because two carpets look the same in the store they will perform the same once installed. Some carpets look new for a long time, others look old within a short time. The difference is in how well they resist soiling and matting. Most carpets do not wear out. They get soiled, change surface texture, and mat, which makes them look old.

Residential Carpets

Residential carpet represents a substantial financial investment for consumers. An informed choice about carpet requires a balance between style requirements and practical considerations. Assess your carpeting requirements by completing the following preliminary carpet needs analysis.

1. What room or rooms will be carpeted?
2. How many square yards of carpet do you need?
   - — Measure the length and the width of each room in feet,
   - — Multiply these numbers together and divide by 9.
   - — Add square yardage numbers for each room. Carpet usually comes in 12-foot rolls. Carpet dealers can help calculate how much carpet you will need if you have an estimate that includes the measurements of the rooms. Make sure the installer remeasures the rooms for a precise calculation.
3. What is your budget? Cost of carpet includes an appropriate pad under the carpet and an amount for installation per square yard. For each carpet sample you consider, get the price per square yard for carpet, pad and installation.
4. Do you need to have old carpet removed? Is there a charge for this service?
5. Are the spaces to be carpeted high, medium or low traffic areas?

Fiber

Table 1 lists the carpet fibers used for residential carpet and their major characteristics. Tufted carpet accounts for the bulk of carpet on today's market. It consists of yarn inserted into a primary backing that creates a pile or three dimensional textile.

Table 1. Properties of fibers used in residential carpeting.

Fiber	Properties
Wool: Expensive, soft feel, luxurious appearance, easy to dye.	Fair abrasion resistance, excellent crush resistance, moderate resistance to stains, attacked by moths, poor sunlight resistance, burns slowly, self-extinguishes in flames.
Nylon: Easy to dye, may have built-in static control; trade Zeftron.	Excellent abrasion and crush resistance, can be manufactured to names: Anso, Antron, Ultron, conceal and resist soil, cleans easily, poor sunlight resistance, burns slowly with melting.
Polyester: Relatively inexpensive, use in moderate to low Pentron, Trevira.	Moderate abrasion resistance, may show some pilling, crush traffic areas; trade names: resistance depends on density, resists water-soluble stains, good sunlight resistance, burns slowly with melting.
Olefin: Can be used indoors and outdoors, light weight, inexpensive; trade names: Marquesa Lana, Genesis.	Excellent abrasion resistance, poor crush resistance, poor sunlight resistance, excellent stain resistance, easy to clean, extremely heat sensitive, burns with melting.

A secondary backing is applied with an adhesive to strengthen and stabilise the carpet. Table 2 shows the three general types of tufted carpet construction: cut pile, loop pile and cut and loop pile.

Table 2. Types of tufted carpet.

Type of Pile	Construction	Characteristics
Cut pile	Saxony plus velour	Individual standing tips, wide range of densities, suitable for most living spaces
Loop pile	Level loop berber	Loops form the surface of the carpet, tend to be very durable
Cut and loop pile	Sculptured	Wide variety of patterns and designs, random patterns tend to hide soil

The following terms describe additional features of tufted carpet.

— *Density*: how tightly carpet fiber or yarn is packed together and bound into the carpet backing.

— *Face weight*: the number of ounces of fiber in a square yard of carpet; applies to the pile yarn.

— *Pile height*: the height of the cut pile yarns or uncut loops when measured from the primary backing.

All three terms are associated with the quality of carpet. High density and high face weight mean more yarn covers the primary backing. The result is increased durability and appearance retention. While longer pile may look luxurious, it crushes more easily. Consumers want to know how a carpet will wear and how it will look over time. You must balance the descriptive characteristics of fiber and construction with the performance criteria required for your needs.

Consult reliable dealers who carry dependable brand names. Ask to see the guarantees before you purchase. Keep track of information from each dealer to make selection easier. Read the labels on the back of carpet samples to determine fiber content, descriptive characteristics and expected performance. By comparing the types of fibers available and assessing your needs, you will be able to make an informed choice about carpet.

Carpets are often classified by the type of fiber used to make surface yarns. On the carpet sample, you will find the generic fiber name used for surface yarns. Advantages and disadvantages of the generic fibers used to make carpeting are listed in the following paragraphs.

Advantages of Acrylic:

— wool-like appearance

— low moisture absorption

— cleans easily

— good stain resistance

— resilient and bulky

— resistant to moths and mildew

— resistant to sunlight damage

Disadvantages of Acrylic:

— not as strong as other synthetics

— produced in short fibers and crimped

— poor resistance to matting

— stained by oil and grease

Advantages of Nylon:

— easy to clean

— extremely strong

— excellent resistance to matting

— available in a wide price range

- good abrasion resistance
- absorbs little moisture
- resists moths, mildew, and fungi
- good stain resistance
- third and fourth generation fibers are anti-static
- fibers modified to hide soiling

Disadvantages of Nylon:

- stained by oil and grease
- degrades and fades in sunlight

Advantages of Olefin (polypropylene):

- easy to clean
- colourfast
- strong fiber
- soil and water resistant
- good stain resistance
- no static problem
- resistant to moths and mildew
- makes good short pile indoor/outdoor carpet

Disadvantages of Olefin (polypropylene):

- depending on construction, tends to mat
- grabs onto oil and grease
- dry-cleaning solvents degrade fibers

Advantages of Polyester:

- soft luxurious feel
- excellent resistance to abrasion
- excellent resistance to mildew
- good stain resistance
- less expensive than nylon

Disadvantages of Polyester:

— prolonged exposure to sunlight weakens fiber

— grabs onto oil and grease

Advantages of Wool:

— crush resistant

— limited pilling problems

— durable

Disadvantages of Wool:

— soils easily

— imported because domestic fibers are finer and weaker

— expensive

Style of a Carpet

The style of a carpet is determined by surface texture. Surface texture has a great deal to do with wearability and the degree of maintenance the carpet will need. The most common carpet surface textures can be divided into three groups: loop piles, cut piles, and combinations. Within each group there are two or three varieties (Figure 2, Carpet Surface Textures). Loop pile consists of yarns that are looped and uncut.

During manufacture, most carpeting starts out as loop pile. Major types of loop pile are level-loop pile and multi-level-loop pile. Both wear well in high traffic areas. The level-loop pile is the same height and uncut, making the carpet surface smooth Textures and level. Levels vary from low and tight construction to a more luxurious high-level loop pile. The multi-level loop pile consists of different height loops, two or three heights being common. This height difference creates a sculptured pattern, which appears to be carved into the carpet surface.

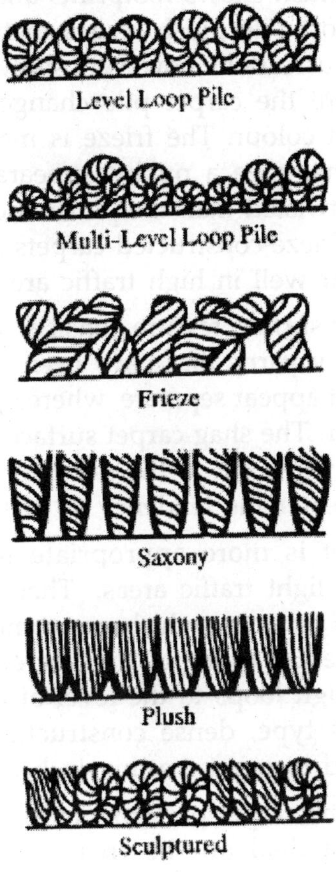

Figure 2. Carpet Surface Textures

The sculpture surfaced texture is often used in a semi-formal atmosphere. A cut pile carpet consists of yarns that are cut at the ends. The differences in the cut pile varieties are largely due to the amount of twist in the yarns. The cut pile falls into four types: velvet or plush, frieze, Saxony, and shag. The plush surface texture consists of yarns cut the same height, which gives a luxurious formal appearance. The plush comes in long pile and short pile.

Long pile plush shows footprints and mats in heavy traffic areas. Short pile plush resists matting better than the long pile plush. Both however, show some shading. Shading is where the carpet pile changes direction and looks a different colour. The frieze is made from tightly twisted yarns that give a nubby appearance. The frieze yarns are more twisted than the plush and do not always point upward. Frieze-constructed carpets are very rugged carpets and wear well in high traffic areas.

The Saxony surface texture consists of dense cut pile made from heavy yarns that have been specially treated to make each tuft appear separate, whereas the plush yarns blend in together. The shag carpet surface texture is made of long twisted yarns cut at the same length. The longer the shag, the greater the tendency to mat.

Shag carpet is more appropriate for an informal atmosphere and light traffic areas. There are also many different surface textures, which are combinations of cut pile and loop pile. For example, tip sheared carpet is made by cutting the high loops to the level of the uncut lower loops. With this type, dense construction and heat set yarns are needed to resist matting in heavy traffic areas.

How well the carpet performs over a period of time depends a great deal on the treatments and finishes applied to the carpet and the way the fiber has been modified to reduce soiling, staining, and a buildup of static electricity. Some of the new fibers called fourth generation fibers have been modified to offer extra soil resistance, anti-static properties, and stain resistance. Many different treatments and finishes are used to make carpets perform better. The anti-static, anti-soil, anti-stain, and anti-microbial are the most common.

Anti-static features are applied during manufacture or after manufacture as a coating on the carpet surface. Antistatic sprays can be applied at home, but these are not as effective as those applied during manufacture. The anti-soil and anti-stain features of a carpet can be achieved by modifying the carpet fiber so it does not show or cling to dirt and stains. Treatments are applied in two ways: during manufacture and after the carpet has been made.

During manufacture anti-soil and anti-stain features may be incorporated into the production of the carpet yarns. After the carpet is made, anti-soil and anti-stain finishes are applied to the carpet surface. Not all of these finishes last forever. Some wear off and some breakdown when the carpet is cleaned. The new anti-microbial treatments prevent growth of bacterial organisms that cause odor. This treatment is applied during the manufacture of the carpet fibers.

Construction Techniques

The three most common types of carpet construction techniques used are tufted, needle-punched, and woven. Carpet construction also includes the way the yarn is put together and what is applied to the back of the carpet. Ninety percent of the carpet constructed today is tufted. Tufted means that hundreds of yarn-threaded needles go through the back of the primary backing fabric to form loops or tufts on the front side. The loops are either cut or left in loops (Figure 3, Carpet Construction). Then the secondary backing is glued to the primary backing to hold the yarns in place and make the carpet stable so it will not stretch out of shape.

The second most common type of carpet construction is called needle punched. Needle punched construction consists of layers of carpet fibers layed onto a fiber mesh, then thousands of needles are punched through the fiber layers to produce a thick, felt-like carpet. The back is coated with a latex material. This type of carpet is very durable in high traffic areas such as kitchens or hallways.

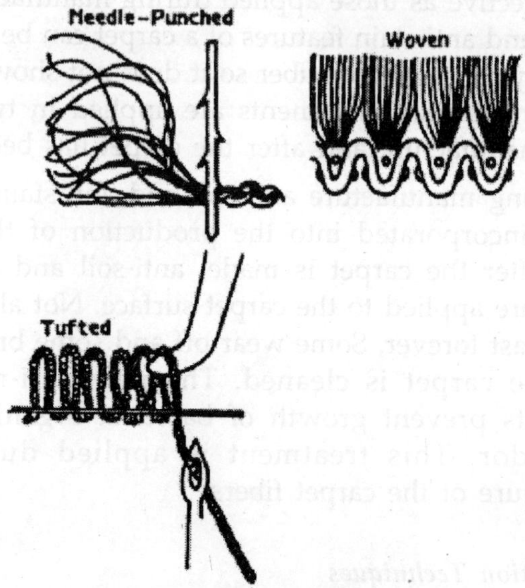

Figure 3. Carpet Construction

Another type of carpet construction found on the market is woven. Woven carpets are made by weaving a surface yarn and backing material into a carpet. It is easy to identify because the carpet rolls only in the direction that it is woven. Woven carpets are uncommon today because of the higher cost due to slower construction. Carpet construction also includes the yarn and how it is constructed. Yarn twist is important in determining quality carpet.

Yarn twist affects a carpet's appearance, durability, and resistance to matting. If the yarn is tightly twisted and heat set, the carpet resists matting and is more durable than the loosely twisted yarn (Figure 4, Yarn Twist). Generally, tightly twisted yarns are denser than loosely twisted yarns because when the yarn is tightly twisted, the diameter gets smaller, which necessitates using more yarns per square inch. The yarn twist must stay twisted to be effective. If the yarn twist unravels, the carpet loses some of its ability to resist matting. Heat setting makes the yarn less likely to unravel.

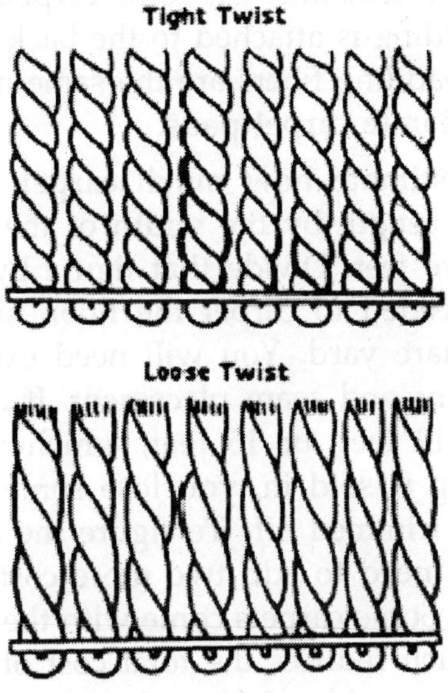

Figure 4. Yarn Twist

Another important part of carpet construction is the back of the carpet. Carpet backing consists of two layers, a primary and secondary backing. The primary backing is found just under the carpet yarns. Some manufacturers colour the primary backing the same as the surface yarns so that the carpet looks denser. The yarns should be firmly attached to the primary backing.

The secondary backing is generally made out of polypropylene, jute, sponge rubber, urethane, or foam, and glued to the primary backing. One disadvantage of jute is that it mildews if damp for a period of time, therefore, carpet with a jute backing should never be put on a concrete floor. Polypropylene (olefin fiber) provides an excellent secondary backing because it is unaffected by moisture, resists mildew growth, and is strong and durable.

The secondary backing can also be made out of sponge rubber or urethane. On some carpets, like kitchen carpets, the padding is attached to the back of the carpet. Some of these padding fibers are the same materials used to make the separate carpet pads.

You can estimate how much carpet you need by multiplying the length by the width of the room in feet to get the square feet. Divide that figure by 9 to get the square yards needed to carpet the floor, since carpet is sold by the square yard. You will need extra carpet for matching patterns and seam placement. If a room is not exactly 9 feet, 12 feet, or 15 feet, which are the usual widths carpeting is sold in, you lose some carpet when the sections are trimmed off. To figure the actual cost of carpet, you will need to add two more costs: carpet pad and installation. Some carpets come with the pad attached to the back, which reduces the total cost of carpeting. A great deal of carpet sold includes a less expensive pad and installation.

Being able to read and understand the carpet sample label helps you know what you are getting for your money. The Textile Fiber Products Identification Act of 1960 requires that the carpet label must list:

1. Manufacturer's register number;
2. Pattern and colour names of the carpet; and
3. Generic fiber name of all surface fibers, in percentages listed according to weight predominance. When the fiber quantity is less than 5%, the label lists "other fibers."

It is important to remember that the Textile Fiber Products Identification Act requires the labeling of carpet pile, not the backing or padding. You may, however, find additional labeling information on the back of the store sample concerning backing, padding, and other carpet features. The dealer is permitted to replace the original label with the store's label if the same information is on the store's label.

Labels may also contain additional information such as: special treatments; anti-soil, anti-static, and anti-stain finishes; type of traffic for which the carpet is intended whether heavy, moderate, or light; and whether the yarn is heat set. Some of the better quality fiber manufacturers have quality control programmes the carpet manufacturer must follow in order to use their fiber. If you are aware of this, the fiber producer's trademark indicates that the carpet manufacturer has met its quality standards. These standards generally include pile density, yarn quality, and in some cases backing quality and construction method.

The label may also indicate that the carpet meets certain standards established by agencies such as the American National Standards Institute and the Carpet and Rug Institute, or government housing agencies such as Housing and Urban Development, Federal Housing Administration, and Farmer's Home Administration. The Flammable Fabrics Act requires that all wall-to-wall carpets meet government flammability standards in order to be sold. It is not required that carpets be labeled since they must meet this standard or they cannot be sold. Scatter and area rugs must also be tested for flammability. If they fail the test, they can still be sold if they are labeled "flammable."

Warranty

A good warranty available on a carpet is a limited warranty for five years. On some carpet warranties, if the wear of the carpet exceeds 10% in five years, the carpet will be replaced. Other warranties indicate that if the carpet shows 10% wear in any one area, the carpet will be replaced. The manufacturer determines this from a sample of your carpet, which is analysed for wear. Some of the less expensive carpets do not have any warranty.

Care and Use

Carpets in a house help to reduce noise levels and minimise heat loss through the floor. They are also more comfortable to lie on or to sit on than a hard wooden floor.

Cleaning

Carpets are harder to clean than bare floors, spilled drinks may stain them, and they tend to collect fur from family pets. They should be vacuumed regularly in order to prevent the accumulation of dust. Carpeting can also be shampooed in order to clean up stains or odors. A good method of getting out tiny particles in carpeting when vaacuming doesn't is to simply use a broom over the affected area. Dust mites can survive very well in carpets, which can be problematic for sufferers of asthma who are allergic to them. Coit Cleaners, a company based in Burlingame California, has devised many sucessful ways of cleaning carpets.

Carpet Pad

Most consumers usually take the carpet pad that is included in the price of the carpet. Sometimes this is not a good idea, since you might be getting a poor quality carpet pad. High-quality carpet pad adds to the life of your carpet by reducing wear and tear. Carpet will last longer if it has a pad. The reason that carpet mats faster without a pad is that greater pressure is put onto the carpet yarns and backing when people walk on the carpet.

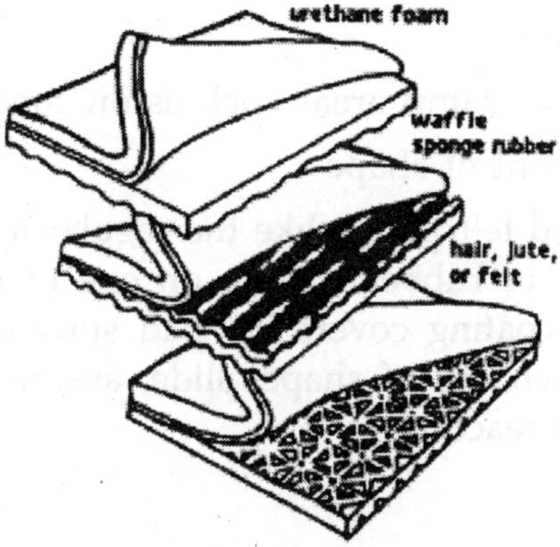

Figure 5. Carpet Pads

There are several varieties of carpet pad on the market. Some are more appropriate in certain circumstances than in others. The most common varieties include felt, rubber, and urethane pads (Figure 5, Carpet Pads). All of these pads are sold in a variety of densities, thicknesses, and weights.

Felt Pads

This pad is made by needle-punching various materials together. Felt pads are made in a variety of ways. Some are made by using 100 percent hair, 100 percent various fibers, or a combination of hair and other fibers. When the hair is combined with jute, the pad is less resilient, absorbs more moisture, and has a shorter life than the 100 percent hair. Some of the characteristics of the felt pad include:

— wears well

— resilient when 100 percent hair

— sheds

— may cause problems to people with allergies
— collects dust
— mildews in damp areas such as on concrete
— stretches out of shape

The rubberized felt pad is like the regular felt pad except it has a latex or rubber coating on one or both sides of the felt. The coating covers the pad surface so it is less likely to stretch out of shape, slide, absorb moisture, or cause allergic reactions.

Foam Rubber

Foam rubber is not exactly the same as real rubber. Foam rubber is made from a latex rubber base, which can be made from different combinations of natural or synthetic latex. It is generally manufactured in flat continuous sheets with a covering on one side for easy installation. This type of pad is often glued to the back of kitchen carpet rather than being a separate pad. When glued to the back of a carpet, the pad is generally thinner and less dense than a separate pad. Characteristics of the foam rubber include:

— insect proof
— mildew and moth proof
— non-allergenic

Sponge Rubber Pad

The flat or waffle sponge rubber pad consists of a combination of natural and/or synthetic rubber and other chemicals. The flat sponge rubber type is made into a continuous sheet. The waffled sponge rubber is first made into a continuous flat sheet, then formed into the waffle shape. Both the flat and waffle sponge have a material glued to the top side for ease of installation. The characteristics of the rubber pad include:

— sensitive to heat
— good resilience
— waffle pad holds moisture
— damaged by dry cleaning solvents
— loss of resilience with age
— moth, beetle, mildew, and mold proof
— non-allergenic

Prime Urethane

Prime urethane is manufactured by a reaction process of polymeric materials. Densified prime urethane is manufactured by changing the cell structure of the prime urethane. Both the prime and densified urethane have a material applied to one or both sides for easy installation. Prime and densified prime carpet pad has the following characteristics:
— non-flammable
— not as resilient as rubber
— not affected by heat
— not affected by dampness or insects
— used on concrete slabs and in basements
— non-allergenic

Bonded Urethane

Bonded urethane is nothing more than little pieces of prime urethane bonded together by pressure and a gluing agent. Characteristics include:
— resistant to heat, dampness, and insects
— not as resilient as rubber or plain urethane
— non-flammable
— used on concrete slab and in basements

Importance of Carpet Pad Thickness

The carpet pad thickness is important. If the pad is too thin, the carpet may look old faster. If the pad is too thick, the carpet is more difficult to stretch when it is being laid and ripples occur over time. The way to select a pad is put it under the carpet you plan to purchase and walk on the two layers to see if it feels too thin or too thick. Another point to consider is to select the pad thickness that fits into the type of room where it will be used.

The thickest carpet pads are used in formal rooms with less traffic. Rooms with the thinner carpet pads are informal rooms with high traffic. Never lay a new carpet pad over an old carpet pad. This makes the layers too thick, which causes ripples.

On the carpet pad sample you should find the name of the manufacturer and the pad name. You may also find the generic name for the fiber used to make the pad. If the generic fiber is not on the sample label, ask the sales clerk. The sales clerk may not know the generic fiber and may have to look it up in the manufacturer's catalog. Knowing the generic fiber name helps you determine if the pad is appropriate for your floor.

You can purchase a carpet pad with a warranty or without a warranty. The better warranties are that the pad will last the life of the carpet placed over it. Some warranties are for the life of two carpets. The carpet pad has to be properly installed for the warranty to be effective. Most warranties are limited, which means that the warranty coverage is reduced according to the number of years since purchase. Make sure you remember to obtain a written copy of the warranty at the time of purchase. Sometimes the sales clerk forgets to give you a copy, so you may have to ask.

7

Carpet Installation

There are six types of floors generally encountered by the commercial installer: below grade concrete, on grade concrete, suspended concrete, suspended wood, terrazzo, and metal. Each of these floor types must be properly prepared to receive both the adhesive and the carpet. Accurate floor preparation is mandatory for a successful adhesive carpet installation. Though some carpet systems are less forgiving than others as to the condition required of the subfloor, every adhered carpet requires a clean, sound substrate.

Concrete Floor Preparation

All cracks 1/8 inch wide or wider must be filled with a suitable Portland Cement-based patch reinforced with polymers. The floor surface must be a sound, dry, clean, smooth, and even plane. Floors must also be free of dust, depressions, protrusions, all existing adhesive, curing agents, parting compounds, oil, grease, paint, sweeping compound residue, and any other contaminant that may prevent the required adhesion of the carpet system backing to the floor.

The 3M Scotch mesh disc driven by a 175 rpm floor machine makes short work of construction related contaminants that must be removed, paint and varnish over spray, joint compound, dried mud, etc. Both sides of the disc are used and the mesh does not load up like sandpaper.

Any adhesive carpet installation over concrete requires a minimum concrete dry density of ninety (90) pounds per cubic foot. Although lightweight concrete (concrete mixed with perlite or vermiculite) may be primed or skim coated to provide a sufficient slab surface density to prevent adhesive absorption into the floor, priming or skim coating will not prevent fractures in the slab surface.

Lightweight concrete surfaces will also be a problem when the carpet is removed. A significant amount of the slab surface may remain attached to the carpet back which has been installed via direct gluedown. Carpet squares pulled up in pressure-sensitive adhesive areas may bring with them from 1/8 to ¼ inch of the slab surface, especially in the heavier trafficked areas.

To check the porosity of a concrete surface, pour a small quantity of water in several test areas. On a good, dense surface, the water will bead up and just sit there. Should the water be absorbed into the floor, the floor is not dense enough. This situation can cause failure of the installation. The same is true in the case of dusty concrete and newly sanded wood floors. When these conditions are encountered, the floor should be primed with a latex primer. Priming will also provide a better adhesive bond and increase the adhesive coverage.

Primers should never be used in an attempt to correct a moisture problem.

Moisture Testing: A moisture test is a requirement for any slab. All on or below grade slabs regardless of the age should be tested. Any moisture test must be performed with a minimum slab temperature of 65°F, because water movement is retarded at lower temperatures and test results will be inaccurate. To test for moisture use the calcium chloride moisture test.

ASTM Designation: F1869-98 Standard Test Method for measuring moisture vapor emission rate of concrete subfloor using Anhydrous Calcium Chloride.

Calcium Chloride Moisture Test: (Conditioning) the test site must be the same temperature and humidity expected during normal use. If this is not possible, then the test conditions should be 75±10°F (23.9±5.5°C) and 50±10% relative humidity. Maintain these conditions 48 hours prior to, and during testing.

Test concrete slabs for moisture using the calcium chloride moisture test. Follow test kit manufacturers instructions. The moisture emission rate of a concrete floor is expressed in Lbs./1000 square feet/24 hours. Approximately 3 days are required for the test. An emission rate of 3.5 lbs. maximum is acceptable. Three test locations are required for areas up to 1000 sq. feet, add one additional test for each 1000 sq. ft. or fraction thereof.

Alkalinity Testing: A pH reading of 5-9.0 is satisfactory. Alkalinity is often a direct result of moisture migrating through the concrete slab. This water movement almost always carries alkaline salts with it and on occasion evidenced by a white residue left on the slab after the moisture evaporates. One may also encounter a hot slab (highly alkaline) which yields no visible signs of alkalinity. Since high alkalinity may cause an adhesive failure, its presence should always be tested for. pH testing must be performed in accordance with ASTM Standard Practice F-710.

Any pH reading above nine (9) will require neutralising the slab with a mild acid solution, followed by a thorough rinsing with water. Moisture and pH test results obtained reflect only the concrete condition at the time. Testing of concrete subfloors for moisture or alkalinity is the responsibility of the owner or general contractor. Testing must be performed by an independent specialist certified by appropriately recognised organisations such as IICRC or EQUAL providing verifiable experience in moisture vapor emission and alkalinity testing.

Other Considerations: Radiant heated floors are concrete slabs into which either electrical or hot water heating coils have been embedded and should present no real problems for a glue-down installation. If the installation is done with the heat on, the temperature of the surface will probably be too warm. If this is the case, adhesive set-up would be accelerated and open-time reduced; therefore, it would be necessary to reduce the floor temperature. The floor temperature must never exceed 85°F.

Painted concrete slabs are hazardous to work with because so many different types of paint are on the market, and many of them are not intended for use with carpet floor adhesives, thus affecting the carpet bond. Or if the adhesive does bond to the paint, the paint in time may release from the floor producing a failure. Wet sanding is the preferred method for removing paint from a concrete slab, followed by thorough porosity testing.

Other surface coatings such as curing compounds, hardeners, sealers, and parting compounds are widely used in new construction and can interfere with the bond of carpet floor adhesives to the slab. Although curing compounds are frequently made of an oil, wax, or resin base and are usually eroded by foot traffic prior to carpet installation, care must be taken to ensure that all residue is removed.

Hardeners do not usually cause trouble, but excess amounts must be removed. In lift-slab and tilt-up construction, parting compounds (intended to prevent adhesion to permit separation of the slabs) must be removed also. If grinding, bead blasting or sanding is necessary to treat any of the above conditions, run a porosity test to determine if a primer is required. The warranties and performance guarantees are the responsibility of the sealer, primer, or underlayment manufacturer and not the carpet manufacturer.

Priming of Concrete and Wood Floors

Priming a subfloor, either concrete or wood, is intended to eliminate, or at least moderate, minor surface dusting. Priming also reinforces the concrete surface, makes adhesive spread easily thus increasing coverage, and improves the adhesive bond.

Priming should never be used to overcome a moisture condition. To prime a subfloor effectively, two coats may be required. The primer may be applied by roller, trowel, or airless at the rate of up to 500 square feet per gallon (depending on the roughness and porosity of the subfloor).

Non-Porous Floor Preparation

Terrazzo and other non-porous floors require a special consideration as subfloors for carpet since the adhesives used depend on evaporation of moisture to achieve a set, which means the water vapor must have a path to the atmosphere. With conventionally backed carpets, evaporation will proceed through the carpet. Endure® Plus, TitanBac™ and Tufloc backed carpets have non-permeable backs, additional opentime considerations need to be made for proper moisture evaporation.

Many resilient floors provide an excellent base for an adhesive carpet system installation if the floors are soundly constructed, securely bonded, free of all finishes, and not cushioned or embossed. Identifying the type construction of the existing resilient floor is critical for insuring successful adhesion.

For example, a securely bonded VAT or VCT floor 3/32 inch minimum thickness provides a good adhesive subfloor; yet, a vinyl floor or rubber floor may not. If it is necessary to adhere to quarry tile, or other tile with recessed grout lines, the floor must be skim coated with a fortified Portland Cement underlayment to bring the grout lines flush and level. Follow the underlayment manufacturer's instructions regarding application, thickness, and priming requirements.

Existing Adhesives

It is strongly recommended that all existing adhesives be removed. An existing carpet latex floor adhesive with the adhesive trowel ridges eliminated can in many cases produce a secure bond. Install several 3' x 3' test areas. Test bond to floor after 72 hours. If extraordinary force is required to pull the carpet from the floor, leaving the floor and carpet back fully covered with adhesive the installation could proceed.

Liquid Adhesive Removers

The use of liquid adhesive removers is not recommended as any residual left on or in the concrete slab is capable of producing a failure of the new floor adhesive. Removal of residual adhesive is recommended by either wet—scraping or by using a terrazzo floor machine. When using a floor machine, use clean sharp, coarse cutting sand mixed with detergent and water. Ensure the mixture stays wet and do not allow any dusting. Thoroughly rinse floor with clear water. Ensure that the concrete slab is thoroughly dry prior to installing the carpet.

Wood Floor Preparation

All existing wood surfaces must be free of chemicals applied under pressure to prevent outdoor deterioration or enhance flame retardancy, oil, wax, paint, varnish, and old adhesives and any other contaminant that may prevent the required adhesion of the carpet backing system to the floor.

Additionally, it is strongly recommended that all wood floors be suspended a minimum of eighteen (18) inches, be cross ventilated, and have an appropriate vapor barrier installed. Wooden subfloors bonded directly to, or laid over, sleepers on concrete that directly contact the ground are not an acceptable substrate for any carpet installation. Possible moisture contained in the concrete can cause the wood to swell, buckle, or eventually rot.

A double-layer wood subfloor suspended over open wood joists (sixteen inches on center or less) and made of ½ inch plywood rated as either APA underlayment INT (interior type), APA underlayment INT (with exterior glue), APA underlayment CC plugged ext. (exterior type), is acceptable as an adhesive subfloor. Single layer tongue and groove with a maximum three (3) inch face should be covered with a ¼ inch APA underlayment grade plywood.

Single layer floors not of tongue and groove construction and having more than a three (3) inch face should be covered with a ½ inch APA underlayment grade plywood. An uncupped, double-layer tongue and groove wood floor is a suitable subfloor for adhesive carpet installations. The warranties and performance guarantees are the responsibility of the plywood or underlayment manufacturer and not the manufacturer of the carpet.

Prior Installation

Before actual installation begins, check the following list to insure compliance with every detail:

Carpet Layout

In order to allow the carpet to become relaxed and conditioned to the room environment, dry lay the carpet in the area a minimum of 24 hours prior to the actual carpet installation. Ensure that the area's temperature is a minimum of 65ºF and the relative humidity is between 10% & 65%.

Carpet adhesive is approved for all direct glue-down installations. The floor adhesive shall be spread uniformly over the subfloor with the correct trowel leaving adhesive ridges of sufficient size to achieve full and complete coverage of the carpet backing.

Seams Preparation and Trimming

Seams shall be prepared by trimming off the mill, or factory edge. This cut is to be made far enough in from the carpet edge so that a clean and even seaming edge is achieved. A minimum of one inch must be trimmed off each edge. Cutting tools with razor-type blades, such as cushion-back cutters, should be used for seam preparation.

All recommendations for seam preparation and cutting must be followed. All edges cut for seaming must be treated with a 1/8 inch bead of Seam sealer. The sealer must be applied along the edge of the carpet at the point where the face yarn goes into the back. Any excess sealer which contaminates the carpet face must be removed immediately using white cotton toweling wet with soap and water.

Loop Pile Constructions: If the carpet is a straight row, level, or multi-level loop construction, insert a row finder, a screwdriver or the nose end of the cushion-back cutter (with the blades retracted) between tuft rows. Run it the entire length of the carpet to be seamed, separating the yarn and opening a path for the cutter. Trim into the body of the carpet far enough from the factory edges to obtain full face weight and good lamination of the backing system.

This distance will vary from a minimum of 1 to 2 inches from the edge on straight row constructions to as much as a 3 inch minimum on some graphic constructions. Using the cushion-back cutter, trim both seam edges by cutting between the tuft rows. Cut close to the main body to obtain a tight seam by trimming with the blade close to the seam edge.

Cut Pile Constructions: Cut pile carpet is sheared in the final stages of manufacturing; therefore, the only thing keeping the cut pile yarn in an erect position is the yarn tuft beside it. Along the factory edges, this face yarn naturally lies to the outside of this edge (no support side). To obtain a uniform pile height on both seam sides, it is always necessary to trim in further on cut piles than on level loops. Depending upon pile height, this distance will range from a minimum of 1 inch to 1 ½ inches into the body of the carpet.

Graphic Constructions: These carpets must be trimmed from the face using either a loop pile cutter or a cushionback cutter. Trim into the body of the carpet far enough from the factory edges to obtain full face weight and good lamination of the backing system.

— Because of the shifting mechanism of graphics tufting equipment, there may be a variance of 2" to 6" in width after selvage edges are trimmed. To separate the rows, use a row finder, cushion-back cutter with the blades retracted or a screwdriver with the blade corners rounded off, and run the instrument the length of the seam.

— Always be sure the blade on the trimmer is on the seam side. This precaution is necessary to prevent trimming the width of the tool beyond the tuft row, thus causing the backing to protrude this distance beyond the face yarn.

— In those situations where tuft rows are not true enough to enable a tuft row on one seam edge to tightly join the tuft row on the opposite seam edge, an alternate seam trimming method is used only on non-pattern constructions.

— This alternative method involves row cutting the first seam edge that has the pile lying toward the seam. Slide the second breadth about 1 ½ inches under the first trimmed edge, or far enough to obtain full face weight. Be sure this overlap is uniform throughout the length of the seam. Using the first trimmed edge as a guide, trace cut the second breadth to the first seam edge. This method is to be used when the edges will not conform when row cut and the carpet does not have a pattern.

For Over Tuft and Printed Patterns: Find the match point (where extra pattern is left on both sides) and cut into the width to the match point-then cut 1 inch into the length. At the match point, you now have a cut shaped like an "L". Perform this trimming procedure at all match points along the entire length of the seam. Turn the previously cut "L's" face up.

Lay a straight edge against the "L's" two at a time. Cut between these two, reset the straight edge between two more "L's", and cut again. (For cut pile carpet, you may want to fold the carpet face down, cut through the secondary back only so as not to bevel cut the face yarn.) This procedure permits you to cut the carpet from the back side and still know where the match is.

Seam Characteristics

Regardless of the seaming method, a properly constructed seam:

- — Has cleanly trimmed edges properly secured with Seam Sealer.
- — Has tightly abutted edges without gaps.
- — Maintains reasonable pattern match where applicable.
- — Will not be invisibile.

INSTRUCTIONS OF INSTALLATION

A high strength, latex-based compound formulated to isolate cutback and other existing adhesives that could affect the bond of the new carpet floor adhesive. In addition, barrier coat prevents plasticizer migration, moisture penetration into the subfloor, and eliminates problems associated with water vapor emissions of up to 10 lbs. of moisture vapor emission over a 1,000 sq. ft. area during a 24-hour period. Barrier coat is non-toxic, has ultralow odor, and is waterproof when dry.

Barrier coat may be used under any conventional flooring system (i.e., carpet, resilient, wood, laminate, and ceramic). Do not use barrier coat under any poured flooring, epoxies, or solid wood.

- — Specifications:
  - — *Approved Floors*: American Plywood Association (A.P.A.) plywood of under layment quality. Concrete above, on, or below grade in the absence of water. May be used over old cutback adhesives, multi-purpose floor adhesives, and pressure sensitive adhesives.
- — *Technical Data*:
  - — *Freeze-thaw*: Protect from freezing; store inside at temperatures between 50°F to 100°F.

  - *Maximum shelf life*: One year at 70°F (if not opened).
  - *Container size*: 4 gallons (US)
- *Typical Coverage*: 100 square yards (900 sq. ft.) per 4 gallon container.
- *Open Time*: Dries to touch in approximately one hour; allow a minimum of 24 hours curing time before spreading adhesive. This elapsed time will allow maximum strength to develop, will prevent the adhesive trowel from cutting the film, and will allow for full chemical and vapor emission resistance.
- *Colour*: Cream
- *Flammability certification class A*: Passes tunnel test ASTM number E84-70 (identical test method to ANS Number 2-5), NFPA number 755, UL number 723, and UBC 42-1.
- *Clean Up*: Use water while barrier coat is still wet. If allowed to dry, it will be necessary to use abrasives to remove barrier coat. Chemical removers have no effect on barrier coat.
- *Limitations*: For professional use only.
- *Site conditions:* The floor temperature must be a minimum of 65°F and the humidity a maximum of 65%. These conditions must be maintained a minimum of 48 hours prior to installation and continually maintained 24 hours a day, 7 days a week and at least 72 hours following completion of the installation.
- *Directions for application over existing adhesives*: Barrier coat provides a protective barrier when used over cut-back, existing carpet adhesives including multipurpose latex, pressure sensitive adhesives, and dried adhesive remover residue. Floors must be dry.
  - *Site conditions*: Concrete floors must be cured and dry.

- *Floor preparation*: All cracks 1/8 inch wide or wider must be filled with a suitable Portland cement-base patch reinforced with polymers. The floor must be free of depressions, protrusions, oil, and grease.
- *Moisture vapor emission testing*: Test all concrete floors for moisture emission rates using anhydrous calcium chloride test kits. An emission rate of 5.0 lbs. or less is acceptable for protection over existing adhesives.
- *Alkalinity testing*: Perform testing in accordance with ASTM Standard Practice F-710. The maximum allowable pH is 11.
- *Application*: Apply with a paint roller designed for textured surfaces. Barrier coat must be applied evenly and without voids. One coat is required. The spread rate is approximately 26 to 35 square yards per gallon.
- *Open time*: Dries to touch in approximately one hour.
- *Curing time*: Barrier coat must be allowed to cure for a minimum of 24 hours before installing the floor covering. This curing time is required in order for it to develop maximum strength preventing the adhesive trowel from cutting the film, and allow for full chemical and vapor emission resistance.

— Directions for barrier coat application for moisture vapor emission control.

- Barrier coat is not to be used over adhesives or any other contaminate when used for vapor emission control.
- *Site conditions*: The site conditions must be in accordance with ASTM. F 1869-98 6 when conducting the moisture vapor emission testing.

— Floor preparation: All cracks 1/8 inch wide or wider must be filled with a suitable Portland cement-base patch reinforced with polymers. The floor surface must be a sound, clean, smooth, and even plane.

The floor must be free of dust, depresssions, protrusions, all existing adhesive, curing agents, parting compounds, sealers, oil, grease, paint, sweeping compound residue, and any other contaminant that may prevent the required adhesion of the barrier coat to the floor.

Cross Seaming

If cross seaming is necessary, insure that the direction of the pile is the same for all pieces and lay each piece into position allowing a minimum of 2 inches overlap at the seam area and 1 ½ inches for trimming at the wall. Trim all lengthwise edges, and fit the trimmed edges to the trimmed edge of the last full width. Reverse roll both seam sides prior to trimming to establish carpet curl towards the floor.

If the carpet will allow, trim the first seam edge of the cross seam between the stitch rows and trace cut the second seam edge to fit the first. Pattern carpet must be matched. A second acceptable method is used when following stitch rows would produce an obvious seam on a slant. Cut the carpet from the face with a cushion back cutter using a straight edge as a guide, trimming the seam edge at a 90° angle to the length seam. Use this trimmed edge (with the pile sweeping toward the seam edge) as a guide for trace cutting the second edge.

Patching

In general, carpet glued directly to the floor lends itself to patching rather than burling. The recommended patching procedure is as follows: For patching purposes, it is best to use a previously installed piece of carpet, if available.

— First, determine pile direction and cut between pile rows, removing the area to be replaced and being careful to avoid cutting the pile yarns. (For cutting purposes, use a slotted blade knife or cushion-back cutter, whichever suits the situation best).

— With an awl, lift out the damaged section and remove any adhesive from the floor.

— Determine the size of the replacement patch by increasing its dimensions slightly as compared to the dimensions of the damaged section of carpeting.

— Apply Carpet Adhesive to the floor and Seam Sealer to edges of the patch.

— Insert the patch by bending the edges inward. Smooth the pile with the back of a knife and finish by tractoring the seam areas.

Pattern Carpet

It is imperative that all parties discuss pattern configuration, the backing system, installation method, bow, skew, and pattern variation to prevent the possibility of having a very dissatisfied customer. All parties must agree upon the expectations of each individual relative to the pattern alignment, pattern impact on quantities and the labour cost to install the patterned carpet. The larger the pattern, the easier to match and install.

Sequence Pattern Carpet by Size: Patterned carpet should be sequenced by the pattern size not by manufacturing roll numbers; however, do not mix dye lots. Patterned carpet is a textile product, and as such, will seldom perfectly match at the seams. The flooring contractor must (a) know what product he is installing prior to opening the carpet at the job site and (b) have the qualified personnel, equipment (power stretchers, etc.) and training to properly install the specified product to the customer's realistic expectations. The goal is to minimise the labour cost in bringing the pattern into register at seams. Install the longest pattern in the dye lot to the next longest pattern—continuing in this manner to the shortest pattern in the dye lot.

- Dry lay the entire area before gluing any carpet; this process allows for documentation of panel sizes and fine-tuning of pattern sequencing.
- As a minimum check, measure the pattern repeat at the open end of each roll. All measurements should be to the nearest ¼". Example 14' 11 ¼", 14' 11 ½", 14' 11 ¾", etc.
  - Measure from an exact match point of the pattern to the corresponding match point in the length direction of the carpet. Measure the pattern nearest the carpet edge.
  - Patterns with length repeat of 7/16" - 3"; count 60 patterns and record the measurement.
  - Patterns with length repeat of 3.1" - 9"; count 20 patterns and record the measurement.
  - Patterns with length repeat of 9.1" - 18"; count 10 patterns and record the measurement.
  - Patterns with length repeat of 18.1" - 48"; count 5 patterns and record the measurement.
- If possible rolls 60' and longer should be checked at openend, roll center, and core end.

Direct Gluedown of Pattern Carpet

Over Tuft and Printed Patterns: Note over tuft and printed patterns do not conform to the carpet tuft rows. Find the match point that is closest to the selvage edge and cut into the width to the match point - then cut 1-inch into the length. At the match point, you now have a cut shaped like an "L". Perform this trimming procedure at all match points along the entire length of both seam sides. Turn the previously cut "L's" face up.

Lay a straight edge against the "L's" two at a time. Using a cushion back cutter trim between these two, reset the straight edge between two more "L's", and cut again. (For cut pile carpet, you may want to fold the carpet face down, cut through the secondary back only so as not to bevel cut the face yarn.) This procedure permits you to cut the carpet from the backside and still know where the match is.

Graphic Patterns/ Techno Weave patterns: Select the match point far enough in from the factory edges to obtain full-face weight and good lamination of the backing system. Tufted patterns are to be row cut so that when the carpet panels are seamed together, the pattern will be completed (i.e., a diamond pattern should be seamtrimmed point to point, thus splitting the diamond into halves).

Run a row finder or a cushion-back cutter with the blades retracted down the length of the selected tuft row. This procedure will open the face yarn and clear a path for easier seam trimming. By staying between the selected tuft row with the cushion-back or loop pile cutter, there will be no deviation from the selected match point as long as the selected tuft row is not crossed. Keep the blade of the seam-trimming tool close to the seam side. Do not trace cut, or double cut pattern carpet having a published pattern repeat.

Stretching-in Patterned Carpet

It is imperative that all parties discuss pattern configuration, the backing system, installation method, bow, skew, and pattern variation to prevent the possibility of having a very dissatisfied customer. All parties must agree upon the expectations of each individual relative to the pattern alignment, pattern impact on quantities and the labour cost to install the pattern carpet.

Pattern Alignment

— Determine seam locations and cut sufficient lengths of carpet to cover the installation area. Be sure to allow for pattern match, plus enough extra carpet along each wall (approximately 2 to 3 inches) for trimming.

— Sequence the cuts, count 30 patterns and compare the measurements to determine the best pattern sequence.

— Align the breadths so the best possible match occurs. Align the rolls working from the largest pattern repeats down to the shortest patterns. Virtually the only way to achieve proper pattern match is to dry lay the entire areas before proceeding.

— Align the pattern along the wall and balance the pattern within the room so the best effect is obtained. For instance, if 1/3 of the pattern is showing on one wall, have 1/3 showing on the opposite wall.

— Should the pattern not match after completing the preceding steps, it will be necessary to power stretch the short pattern to the longer pattern. It is generally better to start in the center of the length of carpet and work the pattern in opposite directions until a match is obtained.

— After the match is obtained in the center of the length of the two breadths to be joined, stay-nail across both widths. Set up the power stretcher so the head of the stretcher will be 2 or 3 feet in front or ahead of the stay-nails on the side with the short pattern. Stretch the short pattern to the long pattern until a match is obtained, and stay-nail the carpet on both sides of the seam to hold the match in place.

Reset the stretcher by moving it 2 or 3 feet and stretch until the two sides match, then stay-nail. The carpet must be stretched at 2 to 3 foot intervals. There are occasions when it will be necessary to swap sides of the seam with the stretcher. The short pattern will be long and the long pattern will become short. For this reason, it is necessary to stay-nail both sides as you power stretch.

— Once the patterns are matched and both edges are butted together, butter both edges with seam sealer. Take the carpet roll core and place it under the seam.

— When the sealer dries, remove the core and seam the carpet together. Allow the adhesive (hot melt or latex) to cure; then remove the stay-nails.

— The area is now ready to power stretch.

Pattern Match Policy

Carpet is a flexible textile material and some degree of shrinkage and/or stretch occurs during the manufacturing process. For this reason, an exact pattern match can not be assured on patterned carpet. The installation of carpet with a pattern requires more time, expense, and expertise than installing carpet with no pattern.

Pattern bow: Maximum bow is 1". To measure, stretch a string across the width of the carpet from match point on one side to the corresponding match point on the opposite side. Measure the match point of the greatest separation from the string.

Pattern skewing: Maximum skew is 1 ¾". This is sometimes referred to as being on the bias. Square the carpet on one end. If the pattern on one side (a) is farther from the squared end than the pattern on the opposite side (b), then the pattern is skewed or on a bias.

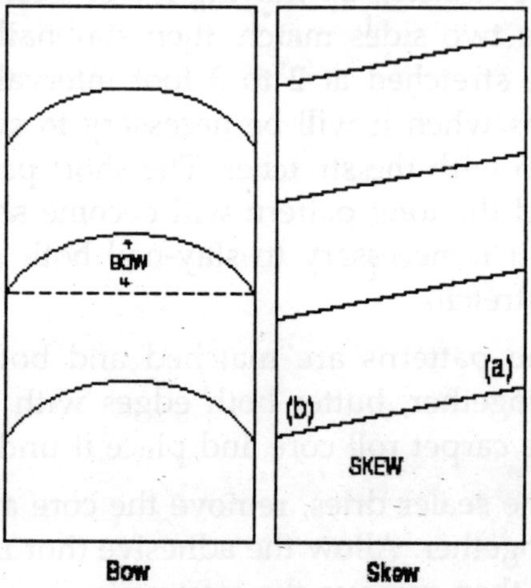

Pattern run off or repeat variation: Maximum lengthwise repeat variation is 2 inches in 15 feet of carpet. Maximum lengthwise repeat variation is 2" in 15 feet of carpet. Exactly match the sequenced carpet pattern at any point along the seam length. The pattern mismatch should be no more than 2" in 15 feet.

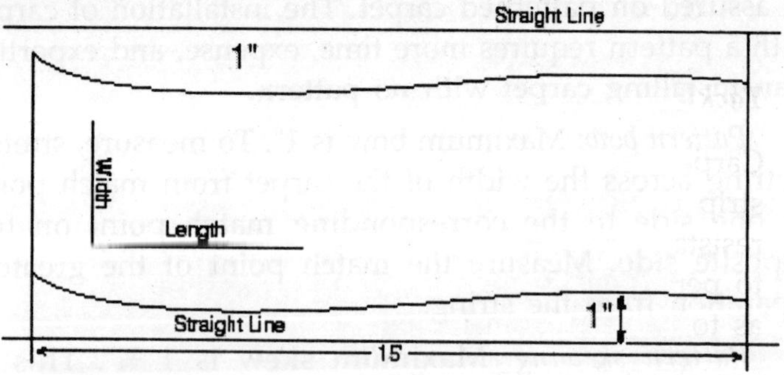

Trueness of edge: Maximum variation is 1" in 15' of length. This is sometimes referred to as serpentine edge. This condition is most visual along the carpet edges, but will to a lesser degree be obvious into the body of the carpet. Do not attempt to correct trueness of edge by cutting the carpet to a straight line. The carpet must be nudged or stretched back into a straight line.

Stop: If you have any doubts about installing this carpet to meet the customer's expectations.

STRETCH-IN INSTALLATIONS

Floor Preparation

- Fill all floor cracks or gaps over ¼" wide with a latex base underlayment.
- Fill and level all low or shallow places with a latex base underlayment.
- Level all high spots or ridges to prevent excessive carpet wear.
- Sweep the area clean.
- Floor temperature must be a minimum of 65°F and relative humidity a maximum of 65% for at least 48 hours prior to installation. Additionally, these conditions should be constantly maintained both during and after installation.

Tackless Strip and Carpet Moldings

Carpet installed over a separate cushion will use a tackless strip of water-resistant plywood with two rows of rust-resistant angular pins. The pins will be of sufficient length to penetrate through the carpet backing, but not so long as to be seen from the surface or to be a safety hazard.

The thickness of the tackless strip will be the minimum suitable for the thickness of the cushion specified; yet, under no circumstances will the dimensions of the tackless strip be less than ¼ inch thick and 1 inch wide. For large areas subjected to heavy traffic, or when any dimension exceeds 30' use a tackless strip with three rows of pins. (Architectural Strip) Install the tackless strip using one of the following methods:

— Pre-nail for wood or concrete floors.

— Adhere with a quality adhesive as recommended by the tackless strip manufacturer.

— Drill and pin by driving square aluminum pins into round holes to form a permanent anchor on an approximately 6-inch center.

Securely fasten the carpet to the tackless strip so that all the pins have penetrated the carpet backing and will hold the carpet stretch. Secure all raw cut edges behind the tackless strip so that no frayed ends or edges show.

Carpet moldings must be specified prior to installation. All carpet moldings will be anchored using the same methods described for installing tackless strips. Carpet moldings used to finish carpet edges in doorways, etc., must be marked on shop drawings and approved by the owner's representative prior to installation.

Cushion Specifications

The cushion should be specified with a scrim, fabric, or film cover. This cover provides a skidable surface so that the cushion will remain in place as the carpet is shifted during installation. This cover also provides sufficient reinforcement to stop the staples from pulling through the cushion. Generally speaking, a carpet cushion which has some give, yet is still firm, is preferable.

A cushion with excessive vertical flexing can produce a loose or wrinkled carpet, split seams, delamination of the secondary backing, foot and leg fatigue, and accelerated wear out. Stretch-in installations will be accomplished by using power stretchers and other devices as necessary to properly stretch the carpet. Installation procedures prior to installation. Before actual installation begins, check the following list to insure compliance with every detail:

— Carpet transported to the job site in rolls free of any wrinkles or creases. Bundling will cause creases and wrinkles which may prove difficult to remove during installation. If loose bundling or bending is absolutely necessary to transport the carpet to the installation site, unroll the carpet as soon as it is delivered.

— Floors properly prepared.

— Building and carpet preconditioned for 48 hours prior to installation at a constant temperature and relative humidi-ty between 65° to 90°F and 35% to 65%, respectively.

— Carpet laid out according to specifications.

— Shop drawing/plan prepared for the area to be carpeted.

— Plan checked against the available roll lengths and dye lot numbers to keep cross seaming to a minimum. If using more that one dye lot, plan the exact seam location where the dye lot change will occur to minimise possible colour differences.

This transition point must be recorded on the shop drawing.

— Plan seam locations so that no perpendicular seams will occur at doorways or entries. All doorway seams should be centered directly under the door.

— Seams should run with the flow of traffic. The only exception occurs when windows allow incoming daylight to highlight seams from the side. In this situation, run the seams into the daylight to reduce the visibility of the seam.

— All seams trimmed.
— Pile running in the same direction.
— All necessary installation equipment available.
— Enough manpower available to professionally complete the installation.

Tackless Strip: Fasten the tackless strip to the floor, leaving a gully or tuck-in space equivalent to about 2/3 of the carpet thickness but not to exceed 3/8 inch. A commercial-rated tackless strip three rows of pins must be used when dimensions exceed 30 feet or in areas designated for Extra Heavy Commercial Traffic.

Separate Cushion: Install cushion in the largest possible lengths using the minimum number of sections. If a foam or sponge cushion is used, all seams must be taped using a minimum 2-inch wide industrial tape. Paper tape is not recommended. A slight stretch must be applied to the cushion to flatten and free it from bubbles and wrinkles. Cushion seams are to be positioned so the carpet seams will not fall directly on them. The cushion is to be trimmed flush to the inside edge of the tackless strip.

For wood subfloors, the cushion must be stapled; random staple through the tape so as not to leave a depressed strip along the seam. On concrete floors, the cushion must be securely adhered to the subfloor with a good quality cushion cement to prevent shifting and buckling.

Protection of the Installation

Traffic over adhesive installation should be restricted for a minimum of 24 hours. Plastic sheeting should not be placed over any carpet installation. Any vapor barrier material may trap moisture, retard adhesive cure, and promote mold and mildew growth.

It is highly recommended that plastic films utilising adhesives should not be used. Adhesive residue may transfer to the carpet surface resulting in rapid soiling. Check with the manufacturer of these protective films for warranty information regarding adhesive transfer and removal. Anytime heavy items are to be rolled over the carpet, protect the installation using sheets of plywood or hardboard in these areas. Modules installed as recommended can be easily lifted and replaced as free lay modules.

— Produces a nice flat installation over trench header ducts, electrical and telephone access covers that are not on a perfect plane with the adjacent floor area.

— Never a need to call back the installers to apply additional adhesive when the traffic for an area changes, for example, from foot traffic to wheeled traffic.

— Moving of furnishings onto a partially completed area will not produce a shifted module field.

— No time consuming lay out of addtional adhesive anchor lines in areas over fifteeen feet.

— Eliminates the need to lay out desk chair positions and other areas requiring a full spread of adhesive.

— Most durable and stable installation method.

— Removes the doubts as to the following questions: Is the adhesive where it needs to be? Are the adhesive anchor lines wide enough? What areas? Where?

— Reduces cupping problems when the building was not quite up to specifications regarding temperature and reduces cupping if the modules are installed too tight.

— There will be no future shifting, producing gaps throughout the installation, should the module field be installed too loose. Each package is labeled to denote style, colour, dye lot, and sequence number.

Dye lots should not be mixed unless specifically authorised by the specifier.

These conditions must be continually maintained 24 hours a day during the module installation. All other construction trades must have their work completed and be out of the area as a clean dust free environment is essential for a successful module installation. Temperature in any module area should never fall below 50°F regardless of the age of the installation.

8

Carpet Maintenance

Every building must have clean, healthy carpet every day. The best place to start with carpet maintenance to reduce time and costs is to keep as much soil as possible out of the building. Placement of walk-off mats outside at heavily used entrances will collect soil from the shoes before it's tracked inside. These mats are especially helpful during rainy weather. It's a good idea to have outside matting, foyer matting, and inside matting. The mats can be cleaned quickly by flushing with a hose or vacuuming.

The mats should be of a construction that will effectively clean and hold soil from shoe soles before it is tracked into the interior carpet surfaces. Consideration should also be given to the carpeting of elevators, even if the entrance lobby is not carpeted. It is certainly wiser to have soil wiped off in the elevator rather than having it tracked over the carpet elsewhere. Watch for areas inside the building that could become trouble spots. Areas in front of vending and soft drink machines should be checked for spills more frequently.

Areas in front of doors leading from concrete surfaces should be vacuumed more frequently to remove concrete dust that will be tracked in. Care should be taken when mopping or refinishing hard surface floors that butt-up to carpet in order not to contaminate the carpet edge. Walk-off mats should be considered for use in these potential trouble spots. Because carpet is the only textile product which must withstand people walking on it continually, it is extremely important that a maintenance plan be in place for every carpet installation. Although consumers would never think about buying an automobile and not taking care of it (clean-up, routine maintenance, and repairs), it's a common belief that all that has to be done to carpet is to vacuum it.

Let's compare carpet maintenance to maintenance of hard surface materials. End-users are fully aware that hard surface must be stripped and polished at recommended intervals. They also understand that after this stripping, polishing, and sealing, people are kept off the surface for a specified amount of time. Carpet deserves the same respect.

Carpet must be vacuumed routinely and extracted at regular intervals. It must be allowed to dry completely before people walk on it. Additionally the mill applied fluorchemical protection must be maintained, and should be tested following each extraction to determine if reapplication is necessary to maintain the effectiveness of the soil resistance, this treatment must be allowed to "cure" before new soil is tracked into the area. There are three key maintenance areas to be considered: preventative maintenance, interim maintenance, and restorative maintenance.

Selection of a Carpet

The appearance of carpet depends upon several factors—colour, pattern, density, fiber, and a viable carpet maintenance programme.

Colour selection

Colour selection is very important. Lighter coloured carpet

shows soil more readily and requires more attention to maintain a high level of appearance. In locations where the soil colour is dark, darker colours of carpet tend to help mask tracked-in soil. In areas where soil is red in colour, a redder hue of carpet will show less soil. However, light colored carpet can be used near shore and beach areas where sand is prevalent.

Darker colored carpet in this case will show sand-colored footprints. Carpeting for restaurants should be in a bold pattern or pronounced tweed. Whatever the case, the carpet will look better and require less attention if the carpet colour and soil colour are compatible.

Density

Density is important in determining how well the carpet will perform and maintain its appearance. If the carpet is made with a loose, lightweight construction, soil can penetrate around the face fibers and down to the backing. The abrasive action of the soil can cut through the fibers, and the soil particles at the base become difficult to remove. A correctly constructed carpet for commercial use is made with the face fibers packed in tightly. Most of the tracked-in soil stays on the surface of a densely constructed carpet where it can be vacuumed away easily.

Patterns

Carpet with a sculptured pattern will require more frequent maintenance in order for the carpet to retain its sculptured appearance. This should be considered at the time the carpet is selected because more frequent vacuuming and pile lifting will be required in order to maintain the pattern definition of the carpet.

Fiber Carpet

The type of fiber in the carpet should be considered,

whether it's a man-made fiber, or a natural fiber like wool. More than 90% of all carpet produced today is manufactured with man-made fibers. Man-made fibers and wools require different types of detergents. Be sure of the fiber content of the carpet before you start any cleaning procedures. The following procedures for effective carpet maintenance have been developed from practical experience and have proven successful when used in conjunction with carpet of appropriate fiber, construction, and colour.

The appropriate selection of carpet colour and construction in addition to the professionalism to establish a proper maintenance programme and the discipline to carry it through will create satisfied carpet users. The use of all cleaning chemicals must be in accordance with proper safety practices, rules, and regulations. The suitability of the products, chemicals, equipment, methods, and procedures for an intended use shall be the responsibility of the user.

Each component of the carpet maintenance system, vacuuming, spotting, and cleaning, must have a positive impact on the indoor air quality; a negative impact is not acceptable. The carpet maintenance procedure selected for any building should be that system which will not adversely impact the interior environment. The products and systems utilised in carpet maintenance must have very low total volatile organic emissions, which will dissipate rapidly.

All equipment must be safe in operation. The system must be capable of safely removing the foreign contaminants which are brought against the carpet in normal service conditions. This includes tracked-in soil, indoor allergens, airborne dust, solids, liquids, or gasses that have contaminated carpet. The carpet maintenance systems and products selected must not distort or damage the carpet face fibers, dyes, texture appearance, or backing system.

Programmed Maintenance

Programmed maintenance is the key to extending the life expectancy of carpet. In fact, the maintenance programme is no less important than the initial carpet specification itself. It used to be that carpet was allowed to soil heavily, almost to the point of no return, before something was done. Research and field testing have revealed that this antiquated approach to carpet cleaning allows abrasive soil particles to build up in the carpet. This shortens the wearlife and abrades synthetic carpet yarns causing the carpet to look much darker and/or dull in those areas, allows spills and stains to remain too long where they become difficult to remove, and diminishes the overall appearance of the carpet.

We are no longer maintaining all areas of our buildings strictly for aesthetics, but are cleaning for a more healthy environment. We now spend the majority of our time living and working indoors. Public buildings and health care facilities especially must be considerate of the most hypersensitive person entering these structures. Carpet cleaning is past history. Taking its place is a new contemporary approach to keep carpet clean, dry, and healthy. Clean carpet looks better, lasts longer and provides great performance.

Today, modern carpet maintenance programming eliminates problems by starting maintenance earlier, performing maintenance operations on a more frequent but less time-consuming schedule, and thereby retaining the carpet's appearance. Remember that one of the advantages of carpet over hard surface is that carpet tends to localise soil. It catches the soil where it occurs, providing a healthier flooring surface. Therefore, considerable time and money can be saved by a programme of planned maintenance in those areas known in advance to be subject to heavier soiling.

Vacuuming

The amount of vacuuming performed should be in direct proportion to the amount and location of traffic. Areas near entryways, lobbies, elevators, and ground floors are considered heavy soiling areas and require more frequent vacuuming. By spending more time on heavily-trafficked areas with a vacuum programme, less soil is tracked farther into the building. Vacuum heavily-trafficked areas with regularity, even if soil is not visible. Carpet vacuums must be capable of removing the dry soil without producing unacceptable pile distortion and without distribution of the particulate or volatile organic chemicals into the air.

High-Efficiency Particulate Air (HEPA) Filters are capable of filtering particles down to micron, which includes bacteria and spores but not viruses. These HEPA-filtered vacuums have a very healthy impact upon indoor air quality. The upright vacuum machine with brush action is effective for soil removal. The action of the brush agitates the pile surface of the carpet and brushes soil from the fibers. The vacuum motor then removes the soil from the carpet. The presence of an adhesive carpet installation system presents a unique situation.

The resultant inability of the carpet to move up to the vacuum cleaner head requires that the cleaner head be able to move down to the carpet. Such installations must be vacuumed with a "carpet groomer" agitator. This agitator has rows of brushes rather than a brush and a beater bar. The larger the area, the larger the vacuum needed. Larger vacuums will get the job done quicker. There are many heavy-duty, large vacuums available that are designed for large areas of carpet.

In addition, smaller commercial machines will be needed for areas where the large machine won't go, such as private offices, and conference rooms. Vacuum bags should be emptied frequently, and never allowed to become more than one-quarter full. As bags fill up, vacuum efficiency decreases. When vacuuming heavy traffic areas, bags should be checked and emptied often. Extra heavy traffic areas such as lobbies, entryways, and areas subjected to immediate off-the-street traffic should be vacuumed one to three times daily depending on the weather.

Vacuum frequency can be determined by visual inspection. Frequent vacuuming in the heavy traffic areas will localise soil. This minimises the amount of soil being tracked into the interior of the building. Heavy Commercial (H.C.) Heavy traffic areas should be vacuumed daily, more if necessary as determined by inspection. Moderate Commercial (M.C.) Moderate traffic areas should be vacuumed daily.

The three carpet maintenance categories are preventative, interim, & restorative.

1. *Preventative*: This category employs the efficient use of walk off mats, carpet protection, viable spotting and vacuuming.
2. *Interim*: This category consists of either Host absorbent compound cleaning, absorbent pad or bonnet method cleaning.
3. *Restorative*: This category entails pile lifting. Pre-spraying as needed and followed by Host absorbent compound extraction, or hot water extraction, and reapplication of carpet protector.

Preventive Maintenance

Mats: It is estimated approximately 85% of dry carpet soil comes in on shoe soles. The preventative category starts with the utilisation of efficient walk-off mats to keep soil out of the building. The minimum mat length should be 15 feet.

Protection: Just as with hard surface flooring, your J&J / Invision comes with a protective finish. Whenever hard surface flooring is stripped, a protective finish is reapplied. Following each carpet extraction, the fluorochemical carpet protector must be checked and maintained.

Caution: Do not use a silicone protector on any J&J / Invision carpet. This will promote accelerated soiling.

Vacuuming: Vacuuming with the correct equipment and frequency is the key to every carpet maintenance system.

SPOTTING

The lifting of spots from the carpet surface will impact the aesthetics of the total carpet area more than any other single factor. Spots should be lifted immediately.

Before attempting to remove a spot or clean a carpet, a pH test should be made on the stained area, and the water and the detergent solution. Testing for pH determines the amount of acid or alkali in soil, water, detergent, and/or chemicals. The reference numbers run from 1 to 14 with 7 being neutral. Anything below 7 is on the acidic side; anything above 7 is on the alkaline side. For instance, white vinegar usually has a reading below a pH of 1; however, it will not burn you. A stronger acid such as sulfuric or muriatic acid can cause considerable damage. The other side of the scale (7 to 14) is relatively safe up to a reading of 10.

Products with a pH above 10 and up to 14 (lye and caustic soda) become highly alkaline. These products can cause burns to humans and total destruction to the carpet.

Since most of the soil in carpet is acidic, detergents are usually alkaline, cleaning solutions with pH range of 4.5-8.5 is safe for wool fiber. A pH no greater than 9 is safe for stain resist nylon, and must be anionic, nonionic or combinations thereof. Do not use cationic cleaning agents. How do you determine the pH factor? Swimming pool and aquarium supply stores usually sell pH testing kits. The kit consists of Hydron paper and a chart that is colour coded.

In order to determine the pH of a spot on the carpet, wet the area to be tested with water that is neutral (7). With a plastic spatula press the Hydron paper to the base of the pile. If the stain or carpet is on the acid side, use an alkaline detergent. If the stain on the carpet is on the alkaline side, use an acid spotter. If your test indicates the carpet is highly alkaline (above 10), use a slightly acidic detergent solution (pH of 4.5-6). Do not go below that reading. To continue to add alkaline to alkaline or acid to acid could cause considerable damage to the carpet. In fact, there have been numerous carpets ruined in this manner.

Spills and spots should be attended to as soon as possible. The longer contaminants remain on the carpet fibers, the harder and more difficult the spots or stains are to remove. Spot cleaning is an important phase of the overall maintenance programme, and when correctly performed, will provide an even, overall appearance to the carpet. Place emphasis on actually removing the spot during the process. Keep the carpet as dry as possible. If loosened too quickly with too much liquid, the foreign matter can run down man-made hydrophobic fibers deeper into the pile.

Spots should be removed daily. Stains differ from spots in that a stain results in a chemical reaction between the soiling material and the carpet face yarn. Some substances, such as acids and strong oxidising agents, may cause such a severe chemical reaction with the carpet pile that they damage, or even destroy the dyes and face yarn. If the carpet installation is large, a special technician may be required for the spot removal programme. This is especially true in health care facilities where the frequency and types of spills are more varied than any other type of carpet installation.

Immediate attention to spots and spills keeps the carpet looking newer longer. Commercial spot cleaning kits are available with several types of spotting agents, detergents, sponges, and brushes. You can also make up your own spot cleaning kit. Since most of the carpet being used today is of man-made fibers, most spills can be removed with a solution of ¼ teaspoon of a liquid dishwashing detergent per 1-cup lukewarm water or Host absorbent compound cleaner.

Oil or grease tracked in from the street or parking lot can be removed with a safety solvent. Caution should be exercised to avoid overwetting. Spot removal solutions and a procedure chart are covered in detail on p. 7-10. If the spill is a soft drink which contained sweetener, the area should be rinsed with a solution of 50% water, 50% white vinegar, then blotted. After blotting, place a stack of white paper towels at least ½ an inch thick over the area and cover with a weight. Capillary action will cause the residue left in the carpet to wick up into the paper towels. This last step is especially helpful when removing spots which reappear following cleaning. The Host compound works well as a blotter.

Locate the spot by name on the spot removal chart. Remove all excess. Scrape up solids with a spatula. Blot up liquids. Do not rub. Apply spot cleaning agents with sponge or white cotton toweling in order listed. Blot with absorbent material or white cotton toweling after each application. When the spot is removed, blot up as much moisture as possible. Place a thick (1/2") layer of white paper towels over the area and weight them down with a heavy object. When the carpet is dry, vacuum to restore the texture. Each of the spot removal materials listed are identified on the spot removal chart by number.

Spot removal is a precise science. Many spots, if addressed immediately and correctly, are easily removed. Coke, coffee, gum, and mud fall into this category. More difficult spots to remove would be nail polish, shoe polish, auto greases, urine, and aged spots. Spots that only a professional cleaner should attempt, either due to the hazardous nature of the required chemicals needed to remove the spot or the permanent damage that improper techniques might produce in the carpet are rust, paints, flooding, medicines, ink, furniture stains, and dyes. Flooding voids manufacturer's warranties.

Spotting Procedures

1. Test the spotting products to be used on a scrap piece of carpet first. If no carpet scrap is available, test in an inconspicuous area. Allow test area to completely dry; then check for any colour change before proceeding. If there is a colour change, do not continue. Pretest additional products until a safe spotting agent is found or call a professional cleaning technician.
2. Remove any dry spill with the use of a spotting brush and bone spatula to scrape up the dry residue. (This process is very efficient for mud, mustard, and ketchup.) Then dry vacuum the area.
3. Blot up wet spills immediately with a white absorbent cotton cloth, a layer of white paper towels, or an absorbent dry cleaning compound.

The Host® Spot Zapper quickly eliminates spots safely (the technician zaps away unsightly spots while standing up.)

1. Sprinkle a small amount of Host Dry Compound on the spot.

2. Using the Host Commercal Spot Zapper, brush the spot north and south, east and west, use short back and forth brushing strokes.
3. Concentrate brushing action on spot. If there is still a trace of the spot, apply a little more Host compound and brush again. When the spot is gone, vacuum.

Wet Spotting

The general rule is that unless you know the origin of the stain and have determined that a wet spotter is required, you should always start with a nonflammable dry cleaning solvent (available through a janitorial supply company.) Work from the outer edge of the spot toward the center to avoid enlarging the spot. Never pour any dry cleaning solvent—or any other liquid cleaner—directly onto the carpet as this causes penetration into the carpet back which can produce buckling and deterioration of the backing system. Rather, pour a small amount of solvent on the white cotton toweling and then gently apply to the spot.

Blot the area with a dry white cotton cloth (or paper towels.) Work the spot by alternately moistening and blotting. When there is no longer any transfer of the spot substance to the cloth, allow the area to dry thoroughly. If any of the spot remains after using the dry cleaning solvent, then work the spot with a wet spotter (e.g., 3M, Host, Bane-Clene, ChemSpec, ServiceMaster, or Tonka Mills) using the same moistening and blotting procedures. Carefully follow the manufacturer's instructions.

Follow the same steps as you did with the dry cleaning solvent. When the stain has been removed, completely rinse the area with tap water to remove spotting agents and any residue. In some carpet colours a slight "white halo" may remain. Immediately vacuum with wet/dry vacuum. Blot with a stack of white paper towels until the moisture is absorbed.

The Spot Came Back: Patience is a must. Do not overwet the spot because you may run the contaminant deeper into the face yarn and into the carpet back. Most heavy liquid spills will work their way back to the carpet pile surface because the carpet back can act as a reservoir for the spill.

Sometimes a spot will return even after it has been removed. This is due to some of the contaminant being left on the carpet back and wicking back to the surface. Or the spotting material has not been rinsed out leaving a sticky residue that collects soil and causes the spot to return. The return of a spot following removal is no reflection on the carpet. Retreating these types of spills and thoroughly rinsing with clear water will eventually eliminate their return.

Chemical Stain: Stains differ from spots. Spots on the carpet are generally a contaminant, or foreign substance that can usually be removed, substantially or completely, by utilising sound spotting techniques. Stains are almost without exception chemicals that have altered or destroyed the carpet dyes, face yarn, or backing material. For example, Benzoyl Peroxide is generally found in acne medications and foot powders. Benzoyl Peroxide requires moisture as a catalyst to trigger the oxidation process. In climates having extended dry seasons, the stain may not appear for months.

High humidity provides sufficient moisture to start the oxidation. Carpet cleaning naturally will do the same. These stains will range in colour from yellow to orange and grow lighter in aging as the carpet dyes are further oxidised. Strong acids are capable of destroying the carpet face yarn and permanently changing the carpet colour.

Bleaches: The chlorine bleaches commonly used in the home and office (5.25-6.00% sodium hypochlorite), even in very diluted forms, will bleach many carpet dyes.

Swimming pool chemicals will produce the same stripping action.

Others: Plant foods, urine, oven cleaners, toilet bowl cleaners, dyes, inks, drain cleaners, mildew removers, insecticides, foot powders, and medicines, are all capable of producing permanent and destructive carpet stains. With the exception of the volatile solvent, all other spotting agents must be completely rinsed from the carpet face yarn as the last step before drying.

Spot Removal For 100 Percent Encore® SD Ultima® Nylon Fibers

One of the outstanding features of Encore® SD Ultima® is that the extrusion process creates fibers with locked-in color resulting in excellent fastness properties. Although Encore® SD Ultima® can be cleaned successfully with general spot cleaning procedures, maintenance personnel—when it is necessary—can use recommended bleach solutions to remove stains which might otherwise be impossible to remove with general spot cleaning techniques.

However, a word of caution is in order: A little bleach goes a long way. Only mild solutions should be used; that is, bleach should be diluted with four parts water per one part household chlorine bleach (5.25-6.00% sodium hypochlorite), and this solution should be left on the carpet only as long as it takes to remove the stain.

Procedures

1. Before attempting to remove the stain, it's important to first test the spotting products to be used on a scrap piece of carpet. If no scrap is available, test an inconspicuous area. Allow the test area to dry completely, then check for any colour change before

proceeding. If there is a colour change, do not continue.

2. Any spill which has dried (e.g., mustard or ketchup) should be removed with the use of a spotting brush and bone spatula by scraping up the dry residue. Then follow the steps listed below and dry vacuum the area.
3. Blot up wet spills with a white absorbent cloth, a layer of white paper towels, or an absorbent compound, e.g., Host compound.
4. The general rule is that unless you know the origin of the stain and have determined that a wet spotter is required, you should always start with a nonflammable dry cleaning solvent (available through a janitorial supply company). Work from the outer edge of the spot toward the center to avoid enlarging the spot. Never pour any dry cleaning solvent—or any other liquid cleaner—directly onto the carpet as this causes penetration into the carpet back which can produce buckling and deterioration of the backing system. Rather, pour a small amount of solvent on the cloth and then gently apply to the spot. Blot the area with a dry white cotton cloth (or white paper towels). Work the spot by alternately moistening and blotting. When there is no longer any transfer of the spot substance to the cloth, allow the area to dry thoroughly. Use the pretested wet spotter in the same moisten and blot technique used with the dry solvent.
5. If a spot or spill remains after step 4, spray with the 4:1 bleach solution. Thoroughly wet the face yarn; however, be careful not to use so much liquid that it saturates the backing. Allow to dry, generally 8 hours.
6. After the area is dry repeat step 5 if the spot or spill is still evident.
7. When the stain has been removed, completely rinse the area with tap water to remove spotting agents and

bleach residue. In some carpet colours, a slight "white halo" may remain. Immediately vacuum with a wet/ dry vacuum. Blot with a stack of white paper towels until moisture is absorbed.

Interim Maintenance

Interim maintenance should involve either Host absorbent compound cleaning traffic lanes and blending into surrounding clean carpet or spray cleaning the carpet surface utilising a maximum 200 RPM rotary floor machine equipped with a drive block assembly and carpet cleaning pad. A fine mist of carpet spray cleaner is applied to the carpet prior to cleaning. Dry time is 20-30 minutes. Traffic Lane Maintenance is a very important factor in the interim carpet maintenance category. After the carpet has been used for a period of time, definite traffic patterns start to appear in traffic areas.

The carpet looks dull, and this dullness is caused by some types of oily soil that cling tightly to the fibers, too tightly in fact, to be removed by regular vacuuming. These traffic lanes should be restored to the same brightness and appearance of the surrounding carpet. Carpet spray cleaning or Host (an absorbent dry cleaning compound made of small organic particles impregnated with water, detergents, and solvents), is applied to the carpet in the areas to be restored. A special machine is used to brush the compound into the carpet.

The brushing action removes soil from the carpet fibers, and the soil attaches itself to the compound particles which are then vacuumed away. The results—the area can be restored by cleaning the traffic lanes and blending the traffic lane edges into the surrounding carpet, by spray cleaning, or absorbent dry cleaning. The Host system is recommended for cut pile or sculptured pattern carpet. Do not spray clean cut pile constructions.

RESTORATIVE MAINTENANCE

Restorative maintenance procedures consist of pile lifting, pre-spraying spots and heavily soiled areas, hot water extraction, or Host Absorbent extraction, and re-application of carpet protector. Maximum allowable dry time for any maintenance procedure is 8 hours. The two factors that dictate cleaning frequencies are the type of use, (i.e., office, school, healthcare), and the traffic classification. These two factors will dictate the frequency of maintenance procedures from vacuuming to overall cleaning.

There is no one cleaning system that fits all facility requirements. Some buildings may find it advantageous to use two extraction systems due to varying use requirements. Level loop constructions in schools and hospitals will usually require more frequent aggressive cleaning than the fine cut pile carpet in the bank president's office. The carpet construction, colour, type of soil, and traffic classification all impact the carpet maintenance frequencies and extraction selection. For great looking healthy carpet, plan your carpet maintenance programme, use the frequency schedule for guidelines, then work your plan.

Preconditioning

Prior to application of any cleaning agent, as much loose soil as possible should be removed. Pile lift the carpet by making one pass in the direction of the pile lay. Then pull the pile lifter backwards so the pile will be lifted and open. This will enhance penetration of the cleaning agent into the pile. If a pile lifter is not available, vacuum the carpet thoroughly. If the area to be cleaned is heavily soiled with any oily or greasy substance, then spray a fine mist of preconditioner over the area five to ten minutes prior to extraction cleaning. The following list shows the most common methods now in use for overall deep cleaning of carpet:

1. Absorbent Compound Extraction
2. Hot Water Extraction

Pretest every cleaning agent. Cleaning carpet with harsh alkaline detergents can be risky. In some cases, dyes might fade. Before using any detergent solution, always pretest on a carpet scrap or in an inconspicuous section of carpet to be sure it will not affect the colour. Allow the test area to completely dry before proceeding. If there is any colour change, stop. Continue to pretest until a safe product is found or call a carpet cleaning professional. The ideal carpet cleaning detergent solution will have the following characteristics:

1. Is environmentally safe
2. Has very low total volatile organic emissions that dissipate quickly
3. Is anionic, nonionic, or combinations thereof.
4. Has a pH of 9 or less
5. Can be used at less than 150°F
6. Has excellent cleaning ability
7. Turns to a crisp powder when dry
8. Will not dull the carpet
9. Will not cause rapid resoil
10. Will not attack dyes
11. Will not be toxic
12. Will not create static electricity
13. Contains no optical brighteners

Pile Setting

Swirls, wand marks, or pile distortion produced by any

carpet maintenance procedure must be immediately eliminated by pile setting or grooming the carpet surface. Carpet must be dry within 8 hours following any maintenance procedure.

Bane Clene Hot Water Extraction Method

The Bane Clene extraction method is an electric truck-mounted system that may be dismounted and brought into high rise buildings, or other buildings for security reasons without any loss of efficiency. Hot water extraction injects the carpet face yarn with a cleaning solution under pressure. The solution is then immediately extracted along with the dirt and grime. Ninety-five percent of the cleaning solution is recovered; therefore, very little moisture is left in the carpet to air dry. The cleaning solution nozzle pressure should be a maximum of 150 P.S.I., which is gentle enough not to damage the carpet pile yarn and low enough not to inject water under carpet modules. The maximum dry time is 2—8 hours.

Host Extraction System

Host's Extraction System very effectively extracts carpet soil. The Host system employs an organic extraction cleaner that is simply sprinkled over the carpet pile and then brushed through it by the Host Liberator®, Freestyle®, or ReliantTM Extraction Machine. Soil and grit are attracted to and absorbed by the Host cleaner, which is then vacuumed away. The Host system is very effective in pile lifting. One of the advantages of this system is that there are no areas out of service waiting for carpet to dry.

Optical Brighteners

Optical brighteners are often commercially added to carpet cleaning agents. These brightening compounds produce a short-term, "artificially clean" appearance by absorbing invisible ultraviolet energy and re-emitting it as visible blue light. Thus the carpet appears brighter and cleaner than it truly is. When exposed to nitrogen oxides in the atmosphere, optical brighteners cause carpet fibers to dull and yellow. This yellowing condition is particularly noticeable on gray colored carpet. Because optical brighteners are a fluorescent dye or whitening agent, the yellow colour is almost impossible to remove safely.

Organic solvents, which might remove the yellow discoloration, cannot be used to treat the carpet because they form explosive mixtures when combined with air. Thus the only sure way to avoid carpet yellowing by optical brighteners is to use carpet cleaning agents which do not contain optical brighteners. J&J Commercial and Invision Carpet Systems strongly discourage the use of optical brighteners for carpet cleaning and will not accept claims resulting from their ill-advised use.

Selection of Caster Wheels

From a maintenance viewpoint the selection of caster wheels is very important.

1. There is a considerable difference in the degree to which casters mark the carpet. Hard rubber casters, for example, appear to impart more of a "dirty" look to the carpet than do some of the hard composition types.
2. Casters with large swivel offsets swivel more easily and wear the carpet less than do those with smaller offsets. Swivel offsets of 1.5 to 2 inches could be used advantageously with 3-inch diameter wheels.
3. Wheels with slightly rounded tread have better carpet wear characteristics than do those with flat tread. When tread is rounded too much, however, the wheel

sinks into the carpet and causes excessive wear because of its limited bearing surface.

4. Ball casters wear carpeting more rapidly than do standard yoke casters.
5. A general rule of thumb is to use soft-wheeled casters on hard surfaces such as vinyl asbestos tile and hard-wheeled casters on soft floorcovering such as commercial carpet.
6. There is little difference between single and dual wheel casters except the styling.
7. Casters having 2.5 inch diameter wheels seem to be good compromises of the various properties desired.

Use chair pads under chairs with roller casters. Carpets with Endure backing require chair pads under rolling casters over seamed areas. Damage from failure to use chair pads under casters as stated above voids warranties.

9

USES AND CLEANING OF RUGS

Rugs are the perfect accessories to really set off our hotel's interior area. They are not only modern and beautiful to look at, but also wonderful to walk and lie on. It reduce noise, especially on hard contemporary flooring like tiles and wood. Area rugs are extremely practical, especially if you like to change the colour scheme or design of your hotel or apartment on a regular basis. An area rug can simply be moved from room to room as your interior develops—much cheaper than replacing a carpet every season!

Area rugs look great on all kinds of flooring, from linoleum to tiles and from slate to wooden floors. Rugs have been produced for thousands of years, and many of the traditional weaving techniques and designs still live on today. A new generation of contemporary rugs to compete with bold accent rugs and complex braided designs are the simple and natural varieties of tropical rugs.

Made with natural plant fibers like bamboo, jute, sisal and sea grass, these products offer excellent value for money and look great within the hotel. The majority of today's rug styles are available in a range of different shapes and sizes.

Abusson Rugs

The Aubusson rug takes its name from the French town of Aubusson, a small, picturesque town situated close to the mountains of the Massif Central and lying on the banks of the River Creuse. Although this medieval town ceased to produce rugs over 130 years ago, it was at one time the very centre of Europe's rug manufacturing industry. The town continues to host a number of tapestry and rug exhibitions each summer. The production of Aubusson rugs is thought to have begun in the seventeenth century and was carried out by a group of skilled, independent weavers who each followed the specific design and style of the Aubusson technique.

This involves interlacing the carpets using a thick-thread weave on large looms to create a flat tapestry with no pile. Along with the French Savonnerie style, also dating back to the 1600's and 1700's, Aubusson rugs are widely regarded as one of the most significant designs to come out of Europe. Indeed, these carpets and tapestries are so popular that they continue to be reproduced in India and Asia. The Savonnerie carpets of this era were only available to the King who very rarely shared his supplies with others.

Persian Rugs

Persian rugs are characterised by their wonderfully rich colours and strong designs and motifs. They are made using either wool or silk threads that are knotted by hand and then backed onto a deep red weave backing. Although many countries around the world use traditional Persian designs, all genuine Persian carpets and rugs are made in Iran and nowhere else. The selection and diversity of Persian rugs is astounding.

Whilst this type of rug can come in all sorts of different shapes and sizes, from the small, delicate tapestries made by hand to the huge carpets produced by expert weavers, you will find that the majority of Persian rugs are made of wool. There are, however, exceptions to this rule. Fine silk was sometimes used to create a carpet for those rich or royal enough to afford it. These silk variations are rather rare and of course very much sought after today. One thing that is certain where a genuine Persian rug is concerned is that, unlike a lot of other rug designs, it will invariably improve with age.

In fact, a rug is regarded as too new if it is less than thirty years old. The Persian rug industry is one that began as a simple trade and developed into an art form. There are a number of periods in history that stand out as significant where the development of Persian rugs and tapestries is concerned. The first, and perhaps the most notable, occurred between 1502 and 1722 during the reign of the Safavid Dynasty, when a number of royal weavers were employed to create new and exciting designs.

The design and colour of your Persian rug depends on its place of manufacture, and each one is named after the particular town in which it was weaved. The Kirman design, for example, is usually made with a very pale red or blue dye and tends to depict one central image or symbol, whilst the Kashan variety is often green or ivory in colour with wonderful curved patterns throughout.

Area Rugs

An area rug can really bring a room together in terms of structure and design. It will allow colour themes and the style of a room's interior to be accentuated by simply repeating these aspects within its design. Area rugs also allow a room's purpose to be defined. Specific areas can be divided up and identified just by placing a rug in the center of that space.

For example, in a very open plan apartment where your living space, eating space and sleeping space are all located within the same four walls, a few well-placed area rugs can immediately define each area as a separate room, thereby giving you a greater feeling of room identity with obvious boundaries determining exactly where one area stops and another one begins.

This technique is also extremely useful when arranging furniture and accessories within a large room, as it helps to divide up the different parts of the area, for example, a seating area could be defined using a very large rug in the centre of the space, with a long runner being used to classify the area from the door to the window as a kind of corridor for people to walk along to get from one side of the room to another.

Wool Area Rugs

You will find that wool area rugs differ greatly in terms of their quality and price. This is due to a number of variable factors, but primarily it is simply down to the many different varieties of sheep's wool that can be used in the production of these rugs. Not only can the wool vary depending on its breed and country of origin, but its age and general health will also help to determine how good the wool is, and ultimately, how much it will cost to buy. Even the manner in which the sheep is sheared can greatly affect the quality of the area rug and how the finished article actually looks.

Area rugs made with wool are thought to be much more durable than those made with alternative materials, thanks to the naturally tough consistency of the substance. They are also considered to be much more robust in terms of looking good, with wool fibers developing an attractive 'patina' as they age, rather than becoming scratched and faded like other synthetic filament. Whilst the rug itself is made up of natural sheep's wool, many so-called wool area rugs will have been made using a synthetic backing to hold the whole thing together.

Round Area Rugs

Round rugs started to be produced in the 1500's. Indeed, the oldest rug of this shape that we know about dates back to this time and originates from Egypt. Its design is known as Mamluk, which consists of a series of complex geometric medallion-like shapes. In this day and age, of course, round rugs have become extremely popular both in the hotel and the office, as well as in many shops and stores. A round rug is often preferred to a square or rectangular rug because its shape is, by definition, free of corners and can therefore be much softer on the eye. The harshness of square corners can look out of place in a lot of the designs associated with today's modern living.

Shag Area Rugs

Shag area rugs and shag-pile carpets are the ultimate in hotel furnishings. Shag-pile rugs come in all different styles—from super trendy and brightly-coloured textured rugs to traditional sheep skin varieties. The majority of shag area rugs are made from nylon, cool or wool (or a combination of the three), however one style that has become increasingly popular with young executives and fans of contemporary furniture is the leather shag rug.

Runner Rugs

A runner rug, often simply referred to as a runner, has many practical as well as aesthetic qualities. Runners not only accentuate and improve the look and feel of a room or hallway by coordinating colours, designs and themes, but they are also great at minimising damage to your original carpet or hardwood floor, as well as helping to insulate the room against heat loss. Because of the long, thin shape of this type of carpet mat, the majority of runner rugs are positioned in narrow areas like hallways, corridors, stairs and kitchens.

However there is no rule to say you should not place your runner in a wider, open area such as a living room or bedroom. If for example, you want to split the room into two defined areas, perhaps with one side allocated to eating and the other side used for socialising, then a runner can be just the thing to help you to achieve this. Alternatively, if you want to encourage people to walk to a particular area within a room, perhaps to another doorway or a window, then a rug runner can help to lead them in the right direction. This technique is particularly useful if you are planning the layout of an office or public area, as it can help to keep people focused and moving in the exact direction in which you want them to go.

Contemporary Rugs

The world of contemporary rugs has evolved greatly from the antique and oriental rugs of centuries ago. Today's industry presents us with an overwhelming range of different colours, shapes and textiles ranging from leather shag piles to tropical designs made of natural fabrics like bamboo and sea grass. If your hotel features a stylish contemporary design, there is nothing better to complement a cool, crisp interior than one of today's modern style rugs.

Choose from luxurious thick pile carpets in beautiful creams and browns, to forward-thinking patterns that really make a statement. For hotels or apartments with exposed floorboards or polished wooden flooring, a contemporary area rug can help to make the room feel welcoming and cozy without imposing upon that wonderful feeling of space that many of us are looking for these days. If you are looking for a rug to complement a slightly more traditionally themed interior, you should not necessarily overlook today's modern designs as a possibility.

Many of the latest rug designs work equally well alongside classic and antique furniture; especially those that have incorporated historical textile patterns and influences, like Chinese and Persian rugs. Modern and designer rug collections are available online, often at greatly reduced prices to those you would find in store.

Braided Rugs

Braided rugs are made using a very simple yet wonderfully effective weaving technique. Traditionally hand woven using scraps and odd-ends of fabric, you will find braided rugs in all manner colours, from sophisticated monotones to exciting mélanges of bright reds, blues and greens. The range of styles and colours mean that they will look good in any room of the hotel. In fact, braided rugs are so versatile that they also look great outdoors on verandas and patios. You may find that some stores refer to braided rugs as rag rugs owing to nature of their humble beginnings, when rags of cloth were literally woven together by hand.

Braided rugs are also sometimes called hooked rugs, a name that is suggestive of the technique used to tie the various pieces of fabric together. When shopping for a braided rug you will come across a wide range of shapes and sizes—including oval, round and rectangular. Try to do your hotelwork beforehand and calculate the exact requirements that you want to fulfill. For instance, if the rug is going to be placed in the centre of a room, totally clear of any objects or furniture, ensure that you measure the area properly and keep a note of these details.

Tropical Rugs

Tropical rugs made with natural materials and fibers are fast-becoming one of the most popular types of rugs, especially amongst young consumers looking for an alternative look for their hotels and apartments. Using leaves and plants to make the hotels more comfortable is hardly a new concept—man has been using them since time began—however incorporating materials like bamboo and sea grass into rugs and carpets is somewhat of a new idea in terms of interior design. There are lots of tropical rugs on the market, all offering different qualities and advantages. You will find that rugs made with natural weaves are much more affordable than carpets made with manmade textiles. They can also be extremely hardwearing, especially if cared for properly.

Bamboo Rugs

Bamboo rugs offer an inexpensive and environmentally-friendly solution to your rug and flooring needs. They can be made from many different varieties of bamboo, from the tall and slender, Semiarundinaria fastuosa, to the Pleioblastus pygmaeus with its small, bluish leaves. The Japanese actually recognise well over a hundred different species of bamboo. Because of the hundreds of different types of bamboo, a bamboo wood rug will be unique and individual. Some area rugs are made with thin reeds which achieve give the rug a light weight and "more flexible" characteristic. Others, however, are made with large and dense stems and actually look more like hardwood flooring than a rug!

Bamboo rugs are suitable for any room in your hotel. Make sure you get a rug with a non-slip backing so it does not move around under foot. If you buy a bamboo rug without a backing be sure to put down a rug pad to keep it in place and to avoid any accidents. Contrary to popular belief, bamboo is a type of grass and not a tree. Because harvesting of bamboo does not involve the actual cropping of the plant itself, its production is extremely safe for the environment. It also grows at an incredible rate so can replenish itself quickly and efficiently. It thrives in warm, tropical climates and is often associated with China, Japan and South East Asia.

Sisal Rugs

Sisal area rugs are relatively inexpensive yet can create a great look if teamed with the right type of furniture. Because sisal rugs are made from plant fibers, you will find that most come in natural colours like cream, light yellow and beige, however some will have a natural red tinge. The most sought after sisal rugs are in fact those that have the lightest colour, as near to pure white as possible. Despite this, it is possible to dye sisal so some suppliers will stock alternative colour options. Sisal rugs are made from the leaves of the 'Agave Sisalana' plant which is native to Central America although now cultivated all over the world.

The plant has wonderfully long, dark green fibrous leaves, perfect for creating a hard wearing rug for the hotel. The fibers are stripped from the leaves, then dried and treated before being woven into beautiful designs, from standard flat weaves in one colour to complex ribbed weaves incorporating a variety of shapes and colours.

Jute Rugs

Jute rugs are similar to sisal rugs in look, design and in their superb versatility. The only real difference is that jute area rugs are made from jute fibers grown in warm, humid climates like China and India, and sisal rugs are made from sisal fiber native to Central America and the

Southern-most states of the US. You may be surprised to learn that jute is one of the most highly produced natural materials in the world. Jute rugs are inexpensive but can help you achieve a lovely, contemporary feel within your hotel.

They tend to be brown or beige in colour with a soft, shiny 'sack-like' texture. Because jute is naturally a smooth fabric, it is advisable to put down a rug pad or some form of underlay first, especially on tiled or slippery wooden flooring. Many manufacturers combine the jute fibers with other textiles like linen and wool to achieve a more durable product. Whilst this will help strengthen the rug from general wear and tear, it will also make it much more porous so is not recommended for outdoor use or in the kitchen or bathroom.

Seagrass Rugs

One of the most interesting and beautiful of all natural fiber rugs, the seagrass rug will quite literally last you a life time. Sea grass is naturally hard wearing thanks to its stiff, non-porous structure. It will not absorb moisture like other tropical rugs can, and is therefore perfect for both indoor and outdoor use. As its name suggests, a sea-grass area rug is made from a grassy fiber which thrives in sea water. Seagrass rugs have a lovely smooth surface which can look amazing in the right room. The perfect place for a sea grass rug is beneath a coffee table or under another eye-catching piece of furniture. The lovely colour and wonderful sheen that the rugs naturally have really helps to 'set-off' an item and will only complement its beauty rather than detract from it.

Oriental Rugs

During the past century, the Oriental rug has become valued throughout the world as a work of art. With its rich history and colour, the Oriental rug often is called the aristocrat of carpets. Although the Oriental rug of today may not soar through the air like the magic carpet of Arabian legend, the Oriental rug does perform magic, transforming interior spaces into extraordinary spaces. The term, Oriental rug, traditionally has been used to describe hand-knotted rugs from the East. The process typically involves stretching warp threads on a loom and knotting the pile to these threads. When a row of knots is completed, a weft thread is inserted.

Once the entire carpet is knotted, the pile is shorn. To a large degree, the precision of the design depends on how tightly the rug has been knotted and how short the pile has been cut. The rug's density, or number of knots per square inch, can be a useful indicator of the fineness and durability of the rug—the more knots the better. A superb Oriental rug may have more than 500 to 1,000 knots per square inch. Historically, the great carpet-producing areas include Turkey, Persia, the Caucasus and Turkestan. Afghanistan, Pakistan, Nepal, India and China also must be added to the list. And under Arab influence, Spain, too, has produced hand-knotted rugs of distinction.

Although there are references to carpets by early Greek and Arab writers, just when the first Oriental rug was woven is unknown. In 1949, a Russian archaeological expedition to the Altai mountains in southern Siberia excavated a royal burial mound that contained a miraculously preserved frozen carpet. Known as the Pazyryk carpet, it was used as a saddle cover for a horse interred in the burial mound. Beautifully designed, the rug dates from the 4th or 5th century B.C. and is the earliest-known surviving example of a hand-knotted carpet. One theory is that the technique of knotting carpets was begun by the nomadic tribes of Central Asia. These tribes produced small rugs typically decorated with geometric motifs inspired by plant and animal forms.

For the nomad, the rugs were both decorative and utilitarian, serving as floor covers, wall hangings, curtains and saddlebags. Because the nomadic carpet-makers were forced to dismantle their looms and move on whenever their security was threatened by natural elements or human foes, their creations may contain irregularities in weave, selvages and design. The wandering nomads are credited with spreading the art of carpet-making to new lands and peoples. Some of the greatest carpet-making centers developed in Persia and Turkey. Persian manuscripts from the reign of Chosroes I, the king of Persia from 531 to 579, describe the Spring Carpet of Chosroes. This rug was woven of wool, silk, gold and silver. It was studded with precious stones.

The period from the 16th century through the first half of the 18th century is known as Persia's golden age of carpet-making. A number of carpets survive from this era and are recognised for their harmony of colours and originality of designs. Carpet-making probably has been taking place in Turkey at least as long as in Persia. After his visit in 1271 to the Turkish region known as Anatolia, Italian traveler Marco Polo described the area's carpets, with their geometric designs and animal figures, as the most beautiful in the world.

Turkish rugs appear frequently in the paintings of well known artists. In fact, German artist Hans Holbein the Younger (1497-1543) painted the geometrically patterned rugs so often that they came to be known in the West as Holbein carpets. It was primarily through Italian merchants that the Oriental rug became recognised and valued in Europe. Venice early established itself as a major trading trader with the East. Venetians spread Oriental rugs along their narrow streets, hung the rugs from windows and used them to decorated their gondolas. By the early 16th century, Oriental rug collections could be found in the great courts of Europe, including those of

Catherine de Medici and Charles V. The Lord Chancellor of England, Cardinal Wolsey, is reported to have purchased 60 Turkish carpets from a Venetian dealer to furnish his palace at Hampton Court.

Western interest in Oriental rugs waned during the 17th and 18th centuries. But after the great exhibition of 1891 in Vienna, Europeans had renewed enthusiasm for the carpets. Americans soon followed suit. Western importers began asking the carpet-makers to modify dimensions, and sometimes colour and design, to satisfy the tastes of Europe and the Americas. In the 20th century, the appeal of the Oriental rug continues to grow.

No matter how well woven and rich in colour, the Oriental rug probably would cease to fascinate without its seemingly infinite variety of designs. Regions develop and jealously guard their own patterns and designs, passing them down from generation to generation. By studying a design, it often is possible to date a carpet and determine where it was produced. To a certain extent, carpet-weaving areas can be divided into those using floral designs and those using geometric shapes and patterns.

Floral patterns dominate in Persia and India. Caucasian and Turkoman rugs almost always employ geometric designs; when the rare floral pattern is used in these rugs, the design tends to be stylised and rectilinear. In Turkey, both floral and geometric designs are used, although the latter are more common. Chinese rugs are easily recognised by patterns that include dragons, monsters or fabulous birds. Most creatures possess symbolic meaning, and, in China, the dragon represents imperial power and also has strong associations with Confucianism.

In Persia, however, the dragon symbolizes evil; in India, death. Scenes of fighting animals on Oriental carpets typically represent the struggle between good and evil.

Plants, flowers, and even geometric motifs, also have special meanings. The cypress tree symbolizes mourning, as well as immortality through death. The palm and the coconut are metaphors of blessing and fulfillment. The peony symbolizes wealth, while the lotus foretells a great lineage. A universal symbol found in South America, Egypt, India and elsewhere is the geometric swastika that has been a popular border design.

In China, the swastika symbolizes peace—a meaning apparently ignored in 20th-century Europe. A frequent Mohammedan symbol is the crescent which signifies faith. Another universal symbol, the endless knot, represents wisdom and immortality. Because the Prophet Mohammed spoke against the artistic representation of humans and animals, geometric patterns often dominate the designs of Islamic peoples. Although Persia embraced the Islamic Shiite religion, the area's carpet-makers often continued to decorate their creations with lively animal and human figures in dream-like surroundings.

On the other hand, it is quite rare to find any animal or human figures on early Turkish rugs. Turkish prayer rugs are characterised by rich and minutely detailed decoration. Found on all prayer rugs is the arched mihrab, or prayer niche, which is pointed to Mecca when the rugs are used in prayer.

The harmonious and radiant colours of the Oriental rug are among its major attractions. It is the richness of the colour scale that allows for the magnificent decorative effects. Prior to the 20th century, traditional dyes—derived from plants and animals—were employed. Recipes were handed down from generation to generation. One of the most important colouring agents was from the madder, a common plant that grows wild in Persia. From the root of the madder came dye for various shades of red and pink.

When combined with a mixture of milk and fermented grape juice, the madder root yielded a violet dye. The bright red cochineal insect also provided red dye, as did the kermes insect that lives in the bark of oak trees. Wild saffron provided a reddish-yellow, while cultivated saffron offered a pure yellow. A lighter yellow came from the root of turmeric. A fungus of the mulberry bush provided a green-yellow. The soaking and fermentation of indigo plants from China and India provided blue. The infrequently used black dye came from iron oxide, and it was the only dye of mineral origin.

However, the acid substance obtained from soaking iron shaving with vinegar can have a corrosive effect on wool. Brown dyes could be made by mixing madder with yellow or from the shells of green walnuts, gallnuts and valonia. The brown dyes sometimes had a tendency to dull with age. The most successful and widely used colours in Oriental rugs are reds, yellows and blues. Red is probably the most popular of all colours and is a favourite of Turkish and Turkistan dyers. Yellow and dark green are used extensively in Persian carpets.

And blue is frequently seen in Caucasian fabrics, particularly those from Armenia. Yarn was not dyed in the skein; instead, each long strand was plunged into the dye. The yarn then was dried in the open air and eventually was exposed to sun and dust. This system imparted to the shades of different strands an endless number of gradations. And these gradations made a woven carpet vibrantly come to life. Around 1870, controversial synthetic dyes came to the coastal regions of the East and eventually worked their way to the nomadic peoples. Particularly for shades of red, the synthetic aniline dyes proved more economical to use than natural dyes. And aniline dyes allowed carpet-makers to speed up production and meet increasing product demand.

Aesthetically, however, the chemical dyes had limited success. Natural dyes mellow with age, while synthetic dyes fade. In some cases, synthetic dyes completely change colour over time. It has been said that naturally dyed carpets become more beautiful with time, but synthetically dyed carpets deteriorate with time. In an attempt to stem the invasion of chemical dyes, Persian sovereign Nasir-ud-din (1848-1896) ordered that all aniline dyes be destroyed. In addition, rugs made with the artificial dyes were confiscated. But smuggling prevented the strict application of these measures.

The laws eventually were modified so that rugs with artificially dyed threads were penalized with an export tax. Since 1920, natural dyes have virtually disappeared from the making of Oriental rugs. The use of synthetic dyes remains controversial. Some say the aniline dyes have been greatly perfected and offer every guarantee of quality. Others say aniline dyes, over time, dry the carpet fibers making them brittle and fragile and seriously diminish the value of modern Oriental rugs.

The material used most often in Oriental rugs is the glossy and supple wool of sheep. Other common materials include goat's hair, camel's hair, cotton and silk. Wool is provided by the numerous flocks, often tended by nomadic shepherds, that graze in vast, undeveloped areas. The finest wool is thought to come from a region, often referred to as Kurdistan, where the western part of Persia borders Turkey. Wool from Khorasan and Kirman is famous for being fine and velvety, while wool from the Caucasus and Central Asia is prized for being strong and lustrous. The nomadic peoples usually shear the animals toward the end of spring. First, the animals are washed by the side of a river or near a well.

The wool undergoes a second washing after the clipping. Then, it is trampled underfoot and dried in the open air. The wool is spun according to age-old methods.

Holding a quantity of wool under arm, the spinner twists the threads and wraps them around a rod. The material for the warp and weft threads varies from region to region. Cotton is used extensively in Persia. In Turkey, particularly in mechanised production, the warp and weft also tend to be of cotton. And the use of cotton for warp and weft threads is increasingly replacing wool in the Caucasus.

Warp threads of goat's hair frequently are found in Afghan, Baluchistan and Bukhara rugs. Because it is not long-wearing, camel's hair has lost favour with the nomads of Turkestan. At times, silk has been used for both the warp and weft threads, giving the rug a sumptuous appearance. Since the silk was expensive and did not wear well, it typically was reserved for carpets woven for holy places, for prayer rugs and for royalty. Sheep's wool continues to be the material of choice for the pile of Oriental rugs. The wool of the pile usually is two-ply, meaning that two threads have been twisted together. It is from the materials used that Oriental rugs obtain their wonderful sheen.

The most basic of looms has been used to produce exquisite Oriental rugs. For the wandering nomads, two trees growing a few feet apart can become a loom when a couple of poles are stretched between the trees. Looms can be horizontal or vertical. Vertical looms are further divided into the village loom, the Tabriz loom and the loom with rollers. The village loom is the simplest with an upper and lower beam, both horizontal, fastened firmly to two vertical posts. The warp threads are rolled around the lower beam and their free ends are brought together in bundles that are fixed to the upper beam.

Whether horizontal or vertical, the loom has a simple mechanism that allows the weaver to divide the warp threads into two sets so that the warp threads can be reversed after each shoot of the weft. The artisan first weaves a selvage. Several shoots of weft are made to obtain a narrow band which is intended as a firm edge for the knotted areas. The knots of yarn are the basis of the carpet's pile. The most common types of knots are the Turkish (Ghiordes) knot and the Persian (Senneh) knot. An important factor in determining a carpet's origin is the identification of the type of knot with which the carpet is tied.

Maintaining

Good Oriental rugs are meant to be used for several generations. It should be noted that, in many eastern countries, shoes are removed before walking on rugs, thereby extending the life cycles of the rugs. Obviously, an Oriental rug in the front foyer will wear faster than a rug in a formal living room with less traffic. Rugs hung on the wall can last for centuries. An Oriental rug should be beaten rarely, if at all. It is preferable to sweep both sides of the carpet with an electric vacuum cleaner.

Brushing the rug against the pile will push dirt deeper into the fabric. Commercial insecticides can be used to guard against moths. It is a good idea to have an Oriental rug examined by an expert annually to check for tears or other problems. If a quality Oriental rug is cleaned and examined regularly, it should remain an object of beauty for years to come.

Rug Cleaning

There are so many excellent rug cleaning products on the market that looking after your rug is easier than ever before. Once you have selected your rug, you'll want to keep it looking as new and beautiful as the day you bought it. The first thing you need to understand is that all rugs are different, and the best way to clean them and the equipment to use will differ from type to type. Despite this there are a couple of basic rules, for example, rotating the rug on a regular basis will minimise wear and tear in specific places. It is also important to use a rug pad to keep the rug in place as this reduces damage caused by excessive movement and friction.

Cleaning Oriental Rugs

— To remove small areas of everyday dirt and spills, get rid of solids and then blot the mark with a clean, dry towel. Alternate this with a cloth soaked in a mixture made of 50% cold water and 50% white vinegar.

— Make sure you get a specialist weaver to undertake any repairs of re-fringing.

Cleaning Sisal and Jute Rugs

— Vacuum regularly to remove everyday grime and dirt.

— You should never shampoo a jute or sisal rug or use a steam cleaner, and always remove spills and moisture with a cloth and a hairdryer.

Cleaning Flokati Rugs

— Restore the fluffiness of your flokati rug by running a garden rake across it.

— If you need to vacuum the rug, only use a suction head, and not a rotating brush as this will damage the wool.

— If it fits in your washing machine it is possible to launder it, but use a mild detergent and a very gentle cycle at a low temperature.

— Never dry your rug in direct sunlight.

— If in doubt, contact a specialist rug cleaner and let them do the work for you!

10

Selection and Maintenance of Curtains

Curtains bring life into a room and are a softer alternative to blinds and shades. They can blend subtly into the rest of the interior or they can be arranged so they become a feature in their own right. A curtain is a piece of cloth intended to block or obscure light. Curtains are often hung on the inside of a building's window to block the travel of light, for instance at night to aid sleeping, or to stop light from escaping outside the building. In this application they are also known as "draperies."

Curtains come in a variety of shapes, materials, sizes, colours and patterns, and they often have their own sections within department stores, whilst some shops are completely dedicated to selling curtains. With the increase in single family homes during the last century, the curtains and drapery industries have witnessed simultaneous growth in the demand for their products. Commercial interests also grew during that time as many companies tried to supply institutions, hotels, and so on. During the second half of the 20th century, many companies profited while others went bankrupt.

Curtains can be very difficult to clean and maintain. Often times they will shrink or tear easily. Also, while

Dry Cleaning curtains, all pins must be removed, then put back in once the process is complete.

Steps for Making Window Curtains

For plain, unpatterned fabrics, texture is important - panels of raw silk or hessian weave have a whole array of textures that just add that little extra detail, while velvet curtains have the uncanny ability to change with the lighting. Bold, contrasting patterns such as stripes look good in a formal setting. Toile de jouy or floral patterns give a room a softer more relaxed.

It is a good idea to have your curtains lined as this will prevent them from fading from continuous exposure to sunlight. Thicker linings can also be added to keep the heat from escaping the room—they can act as a kind of insulating layer. Lined curtains will be significantly heavier and may require a sturdier support system. Making your own curtains enables you to colour co-ordinate your room and even match the curtains with the cushions or tablecloth if you desire. The initial idea may seem a little daunting but don't be put off. If you can use a sewing machine and sew in a straight line, making your own curtains is not difficult and can be a satisfying project. Unlined curtains with metal or plastic hooks to attach to the curtain pole are the most straightforward to make and so a good place for a beginner to start.

Measuring the Windows

This is first step to make a window curtain. When taking measurements for curtains you need to be very exact. It would be pretty disappointing to proudly hang your curtains only to find they're an inch too short. When measuring for the length of the curtains, take the measurements from the curtain pole to the bottom of the window. You need to add on 8 inches to the total height measurement to allow for hems. As you want your curtains to be gathered when shut and not pulled taught across the window, double the width measurement of your window and add 8 inches for seams to get your ideal width.

Choosing the Fabric

Second step is choosing the fabrics. As you'll be making unlines curtains, it's important to choose good quality material in an appropriate colour. If you are making unlined curtains for a bedroom for example, you won't be thanked for making them in white. Fabrics come in two widths, 45 and 60 inches. This is wide enough to fit all standard windows; if your windows are unusually large, you might need to buy two widths and stitch them together. When purchasing the material, round up any measurements, as it's always better to have too much than too little. Cut the material in half to create the two curtain panels.

Making the Curtains

Step three: Lay out the fabric on a flat surface with the right side facing down. Turn a double 1-inch hem at each side, pin in place, then stitch. Turn a double 3-inch hem at the bottom, and do the same. Remember to use a ruler or tape measure to ensure your measurements are accurate. A strip of heading tape into which the hooks will go needs to be sewn at the top of the curtain. The best way to attach this is to turn down 2 inches at the top, lay the heading tape on top of this and stitch both in place at the same time. The curtain hooks are then looped into the heading tape and your curtain is ready for hanging.

Adding Style and Atmosphere of Window

Glass window panes allow the light into our houses and give us a view of the outside world. However glass does not keep the heat in and also allows passersby to look in depriving us of our privacy. Window curtains have the practical function of keeping the light out and the warmth in. The most common form of window curtains are two panels which hang either side of the window frame when open and can be pulled shut to cover the whole window. Single panels cover the whole window and can be held to one side with tiebacks. The panels can be gathered or pleated at the top so they fall in folds. Windows which have radiators under the sills should have drapes which come to just below the sill to allow the heat to circulate round the room.

Floor-length window curtains look very smart but absorb the heat from radiators. Drapes with large patterns, such as toile, need to be used for large windows to avoid breaking up the interwoven pattern. Sheer curtains allow the light in and can therefore be left covering the window as a permanent fixture. Heavier materials such as velvet are a snug choice for the bedroom as they don't let the warmth flow out and they achieve a nearly complete "Blackout" state—great for light sleep. Lighter fabrics work better in bathrooms as they are less prone to retaining moisture and going moldy. Cotton drapes work well in bathrooms, kitchens or in kids' rooms as no fuss needs to be made when it comes to washing—simply bung them in the machine on a regular wash.

Bay windows consist of three window panes with the two side panes angled to form the bay. Bay window curtains are usually attached using track which has been bent to fit the window. Arched windows can also present a little difficulty. They can be fitted with clear rods shaped to fit the window which can then be used to hang a lace curtain or other decorative window treatment. For particularly awkward windows, it may be worth considering having custom curtains made. Ready-made curtains are available in different styles and fabrics and provide an affordable and practical solution to most window dressing problems (if anything else that at least provide you with some stall time till you decide on what you really want.)

Windows allow us to look out onto the world while bringing life and light into our homes. Using the correct window treatments can maximise the beauty of your windows; chosen well, the right curtains, blinds and window hardware lends style and atmosphere to any room. Compare how luscious velvet drapes reflect the grandness of a manor house while a beach bungalow benefits from light, airy sheers that billow with the breeze. Bright yellow curtains cheer up a kitchen while simple black valances keep small bathrooms neutral; lace can be flirtatious while corduroy lends an earthy feeling.

Curtain rods are easily hidden while curtain poles capped with end finials are decoration in themselves. Choosing the best window treatments for your home requires a little more work than simply picking the colour of a curtain. Understanding window décor depends on a number of considerations:

— You must embrace any limitations caused by the shape and style of your windows. For example, a single square window placed in the center of a wall should be approached differently than a set of French doors or a pair of mismatched windows; bay windows, on the other hand, present a different challenge as their angles cancel out many pieces of standard window hardware.

— You must prioritise your needs. Maybe you live on a busy street and privacy is a main concern. Southern exposure windows may require an additional measure of light control. Perhaps you need to insulate a set of drafty windows or doors. Window treatments can be customised to fit any dimensions as well as provide special features such as remote control operation, solar heating panels and cordless control.

Choosing your window treatments also means understanding and accepting the four facets of window treatment design:

— Fabric is a major decision. Not only will your fabric convey a certain attitude (i.e. velvet is much more formal than cotton) but it must be of the right weight to balance with your window.
— How you attach the window treatments to the window is also important; rods, poles and rings are all unique elements of design.
— Choosing the right heading to complement your treatment can add style and flair or cause a fashion disaster.

Finishing off your window treatments with embellishments requires a bit of design awareness; for example, you never want to make a modern window treatment appear too fussy with excess additions.

Window Treatment Design

Window treatment design is about more than just curtains and blinds; in fact, four elements of style are responsible for adding atmosphere and interest no matter the motif. The ability to customise each of the four elements, from the fabric and support to the heading and embellishments, allows you to control how your widow treatment impacts the room.

Fabric is the most important and defining part of any window treatment. A formal dining room comes together with the addition of a pair of rich damask drapes while a sunny kitchen fares better with light cotton. When deciding on a window treatment design, be aware that fabric depends on three aspects; colour, weight and pattern. Colour is integral to defining your design; warm and earthy shades add coziness while cool colors come across as 'crisp.' The weight of the fabric makes a different statement; heavy curtains frame an area to impart a reserved air while lighter ones billow and open up a living area. Pattern is the last aspect.

Plain, textured fabrics are generally less noticeable than those that carry a design, but subtle patterns recede more than striking colors do. Support is the second element of any window treatment design. There are a few things to consider when choosing your attachments; Analyse your fabric and verify that its weight and design matches the support; wool curtains might be too heavy for a thin track while a heavy pole can carry attention away from delicate sheers. Hidden tracks and curtain rods are generally less noticeable support while poles can be quite decorative, especially with the addition of end finials and curtain rings. Heading is considered similar to support but is truly its own individual design element. The heading controls how your fabric hangs and while concealing the support.

Stiff pencil pleats and French pleats can be gathered across a curtain rod to impart fancy formality while a simple slot heading allows a curtain to slide easily across a rod. Rings and pleats are paired for decoration while a pole adds extra flair and ruffles and eyelets are distinct in their own manner. Embellishment is the last aspect to take into account; use them to give your window treatment design that extra bit of unique flair. Embellishment ranges from simple drapes and folds in the fabric to fanciful hand-made lace borders and dangling charms. They can be purely decorative in the form of tassels, buttons and fringes, or provide function through ties, loops and tassels.

French Door Window Treatment

French doors are a beautiful accent to any home, infusing rooms with distinct style while bringing in light and air. It is essential to find the right French door window treatments to foster, rather than diminish, their unique appeal; however, this doesn't mean wading through stacks of curtains, rods and blinds. Here's some advice on how to dress your French doors. French doors are designed to be used. They allow access to a deck, veranda or even another room by swinging outwards or inwards on hinges. This makes finding appropriate French door window treatments a bit more difficult, as you never want to block the doorway or obstruct the hinge mechanism from functioning properly.

There are always solutions for decorating your French doors. Door panels in sheer or solid curtains are a popular choice; gather them on poles at the bottom and top of the window and then draw the fabric together in the middle to resemble an hour glass shape. This lets in a bit of light while allowing some privacy; the panels may then be drawn outwards again to cover more of the window. Thin, sheer curtains work especially well with French doors provided that they are on a curtain rod or pole long enough to hold the fabric clear of the doors. In fact, it can be quite pleasant to open a set of French doors, draw a pair of sheer curtains and allow the breeze to send them sailing breezily into the room.

If you're searching for more privacy, full-size indoor shutters on a track can be a great choice. Slide them along the tracks to open and close; when placed across French doors these wooden shutters afford maximum privacy and security. If you prefer to use window treatments that are not the same size of the doors, try a set of plantation shutters. These attractive wooden shutter tilt up and down to close are also another good option.

Your neighbourhood fabric and craft store is a good place to go if you have questions about material. Visit a local home improvement store for suggestions on hardware; home furnishing stores usually carry a great assortment of shades and blinds in their window treatment departments.

Bay Window Treatments

Bay windows make a beautiful and unique accent to any home, but using the wrong window treatment will only diminish their natural appeal. On the other hand, the right bay window treatments will highlight, illuminate and bring the sparkle out of your window.

Bay windows are unique with their three dimensional, three window design as the additional angles make it hard to find headings. Curtain rods and poles can be used, but they must be bought and installed individually in three different sets. This tends to throw a lot of designers off track. It's best to stick to simple window treatments because decorating a bay window with multiple blinds or curtains will appear fussy and overly complicated.

There are a few options for bay window treatments; some people find success with a curved track that follows the angling of the window. A single or double set of curtains can then be drawn across the continuous track. Be prepared to use power tools or to enlist extra help when choosing this option, for bending the metal curtain rod into the same shape as the window can requires a bit of manpower and/or expense. Another suggestion is to use three separate, solid shades that gather up into themselves at the top of the window.

As for curtains, simple swags or Roman curtains are the best option because they can be easily affixed to each individual window. If you prefer to have long drapes, plan to install a curtain rod or pole across the top of the bay window on the wall facing into the room. A curtain scarf looped on and around a decorative curtain pole is a good solution; cap the ends of the poles with carved finials and voila! A simple yet decorative solution.

Kitchen Window Treatments

Kitchens aren't just for cooking anymore. Today they can be a stylish centerpiece, the hub of family life or even an area devoted to entertaining. As more attention is paid to their design, installing the perfect kitchen window treatments becomes essential for conveying atmosphere. Not just any old curtain or window hardware will suffice when striving for the ideal kitchen décor. Choosing your kitchen window treatments depends on the style of kitchen you have; here are the best window treatment suggestions organised by decorating theme:

Country kitchens are back in vogue. Evoking a pleasant, homey feeling, country style ranges from bright and simple to cluttered and cozy. Try small floral or fruit patterns and coloured block checks in a set of tab curtains or balloon valance. Fabrics such as muslin, cotton, canvas and woven fabrics work well. Or skip curtains altogether and place a carved wooden shelf above the window, then decorate with copper pots or garland.

Celebrate sleek and modern; maximise the impact of tile and stainless steel by integrating your kitchen window treatments into your contemporary décor. Simple curtain designs are best for maintaining the 'clean' look; let in the light with sheer fabrics such as treated or raw silk and muslin. Bright primary colors and geometric patterns work well or add some texture with corduroy and canvas.

A simple pull shade will quietly blend in while a Roman shade adds decorative flair. Or affix a set of glass shelves onto the window and place a couple of clear, coloured glass objects onto them.

Try cherry prints or vines and small hanging mini-drapes; finish your curtain rods and poles in lacquer and enamel. For a funky 'diner style,' hang up a pair of café curtains. Complete the look by hanging retro pictures and prints alongside the window.

Old European kitchens provide a unique yet popular style. Try traditional Laura Ashley florals, ruffled valances and white shutters for an English air. Invoke the warmth and bustle of an Italian country kitchen by hanging strands of garlic and peppers in large windows. Stick to washed out shades of warm colors. French subtlety can be conveyed through shades of white and blue, bistro curtains and brass curtain rods. Spanish influence is supplied by deep, warm colors such as maroon and burnt sienna, decorative wall tiles and embroidered panels.

DIY Patterns of Window Treatment

Although variety is a good thing when it comes to home decorating, even the greatest amount of choice doesn't guarantee you'll find exactly what you're looking for. On the bright side, it is relatively easy to create and prepare your own window treatment patterns, provided you keep these considerations in mind:

— *Complication*. How difficult or simple do you want your window treatment to be? Café curtains, which are basically two pieces of fabric strung across the window at the window's midpoint, are very easy to make and only require a basic curtain rod. On the other hand, lambrequins and goblet-pleated puddle drapes demand more extensive time and effort. Keep in mind that the more involved your window treatment patterns, the more energy and money you may have to spend to accomplish the look you want.

— *Cost*: Ask yourself how much you are planning to spend. Do your window treatment patterns involve expensive components such as fancy drapes, brass curtain rods or carved wooden finials? Pairing solid curtains with sheers doubles your cost. Adding trim and other notions also increases the amount of money you should plan to spend. Simple fabrics such as cotton and polyester blends are less expensive than richer ones and metal and wood window hardware drives up the cost more so than plastic.

— *Directions*: Illusions of grandeur are easily shot down with the realisation that you don't understand the directions or the terminology. Make sure your chosen window treatment pattern makes it perfectly clear what you should be buying and/or doing in order to achieve your desired look. It's never a good thing when you are half done and realise that you bought a socket bracket when what you really needed was a spool rod.

— *Measuring*: Remember the old saying, 'measure twice and cut once.' Be precise in all your measurements; many window treatment patterns purposefully require you to leave some 'extra room' for the eventual gathering or draping of the fabric. Fabric can also be one of the most expensive components of the window treatment; cutting corners when measuring will only result in you cutting the material incorrectly.

Custom Window Treatments

Sometimes having too many choices can be more frustrating than not having enough. The wide array of window decorating options and accessories can be mind-boggling, yet even a wide assortment of goods doesn't guarantee you'll find exactly what you're looking for. If you're stumped for decorating ideas, it can be a good idea to look into custom window treatments.

Whoever said all windows are created equal? Many people order custom window treatments to cover oddly shaped or hard-to-fit windows. Others simply want their decorating schemes to remain unique. Of course, it's always hassle-free to leave your window treatment responsibilities to the experts. No matter your reasoning, it's easy to order custom measured and designed window treatments; all you need to know is where to look. A number of companies offer custom window treatments.

Not only can customers specify their own dimensions, but they may choose from among a wide variety of additional features such as remote-controlled shades, special tinting and cordless blinds. Simply contact one of the following stores to talk to a designer, order a free brochure or catalogue, or to visit a store in person.

Cost Cutting Tips

Decorating your home can be a satisfying though somewhat expensive process. However, there's no reason to break the bank in the name of style when discount window treatments are easy to find and easy on the wallet, providing a great solution for any do-it-yourself designer. First you have to know what you're looking for when choosing window treatment accessories. Keep in mind that style and quality reflect the cost of the window accessory:

— Plastic curtain rods are less expensive than metal ones. Shower curtain rods can be a cost-conscious substitute, especially covered and hidden by the curtain fabric.

— Curtain poles are more aesthetic and cost more than rods. Available in carved wood and metal, poles affix to the wall via hooks or decorative wooden attachments.

— Carved wooden end finials (the decorative caps that fit over the ends of the curtain rods) can be expensive, depending on how intricate the design.

— When choosing curtains, remember that the more fabric you need, the more money you should expect to spend. For example, long panels are more expensive than short valances and shades.

— The type of fabric you choose also changes the price; stick to simple patterns and inexpensive cottons and percale blends to save money.

Know where to look for an assortment of discount window treatments. Commercial home improvement stores and large retail chains are great places to find any accessory from curtain ring to rod. Known for stocking a variety of styles, brands and price levels, superstores offer customers plenty of options. Their wide selection allows you to purchase everything you need in one shopping trip, plus knowledgeable sales people are available to answer any questions you may have.

It is a good idea to browse through the clearance sections of window departments when searching for discount prices. Retailers promote the sale of their overstock by offering buyers incentives such as reduced prices or two-for-one deals. Sometimes the best discount window treatments are found at home. With a bit of creativity and craftiness anyone can create a number of basic window accessories.

— If you can't find curtain rings, use ribbon, tying the ends off into bows. Other options include metal washers and inexpensive hooks.

— Visit your local hardware store and substitute a large wooden dowel for a curtain rod. These unfinished wood poles vary in thickness and length and can be finished with stain or varnish.

— Visit a factory outlet store for great deals on curtain fabric or buy your fabric in bulk from an online store.
— If you want cotton curtains, flat bed sheets can make a great substitute. Grab a pair to make a set of long panels or cut and hem for a valance.

Types of Curtains

Bamboo Curtains

Bring the spirit of aloha into your home with hand-painted bamboo curtains. As a souvenir of a magical vacation in Hawaii, or simply a style choice, bamboo curtains are an attractive accessory in any home. What's so great about this material is that it is an environmentally-friendly, and because bamboo grows very quickly it is a realistically replenish able resource. This beautiful, lightweight material is ideal for attractive curtains all round the house. People use them as door curtains, window curtains, wall hangings or put them over a closet instead of doors. Bamboo curtains are not commonplace and are often only stocked by specialist vendors

Bamboo curtains bring a touch of the tropics into your home. Their Hawaiian origins are reflected in some of the designs available: a crouched surfer riding a wave, a palm tree in front of a setting sun. The curtains are made of pieces of bamboo which are about half inch wide and are stuck together to form a surface for hand-painting or printing a design on. They are attached to a wooden slat which runs across the top and has eyelets to make the curtains easy to put up. Other designs that would appeal to children in particular are available such as mermaids or animals such as cats or dolphins.

Beaded bamboo curtains: Long, cylindrical bamboo beads are strung together on threads and attached to a wooden slat across the top. Bamboo is easy to dye and different-coloured beads are used on the strands to form a pattern. As bamboo is lightweight it is a good material for making door curtains. The hollow beads make a knocking noise as they are moved by the wind or by someone brushing through the strands aside - an unobtrusive and somewhat calming sound.

Installing bamboo curtains is not a complicated process as they are usually attached to a wood frame with eyelets. Hold up the frame and make sure it is level above the door or window where it is to go. It is better to do it by eye in case the door or window frame is not completely level. Mark where the curtain hooks need to go with a pencil and then hammer in the hooks in. The curtain eyelets should fit over hooks. You may need to trim your curtain to fit the doorway or window. Trim carefully—do not take too much off, if you take too little off you can always trim some more off but once you have gone too far you can not stick it back on!

Toile Curtains

Toile curtains are a popular choice for a peaceful, rustic look in your home. Toile refers to the pattern used on the material and toile was first produced in the French town of Jouy in the 18th century. Therefore toile can also be referred to as toile de jouy. Plants, animals, flowers and country scenes such as deer drinking out of rivers were printed on cotton fabric. Originally the designs would use just one colour on a plain background but later on multicoloured designs started appearing. French toile curtains usually have a coloured pattern in colors such as red, blue or green on a white or cream background but there are some unusual variations available such as a red pattern on a gold background.

Toile curtains are produced in different fabrics these days including plastic—yes you even get "toiled" shower curtains! French toile curtains add peace and charm to a bedroom or kitchen. The style of pattern is not intrusive and goes with most types rustic / country themed decor. Remember when using patterned fabric that a large pattern on a small window won't be seen properly—it will appear broken up and "bitsy". This type of pattern consists of scenes that need to be seen as a whole to make sense and would therefore suit a large space such as floor-length curtains for French windows.

Another consideration is whether you would like the drapes lined or not. Sheer curtains allow the light through which shows the pattern up but lined toile curtains allow the design to be seen more clearly. The other advantage of lined curtains is that the lining prevents the pattern from fading in the sun.

Sheer Curtains

Sheer curtains are translucent drapes which cover a window while allowing the maximum amount light to still stream through, meaning the curtains can be kept closed. Their purpose is to screen largely to add "some" privacy while not cutting the room off from any beauty emanating in from the outside. Sheer drapes are made of fine, delicate fabric so they allow daylight into the room while ensuring privacy. Any sort of open-weave fabric will fulfill this purpose—net or lace curtains are popular in most suburban homes.

A great alternative for those who want plain drapes without any pattern or frills is muslin, a thin fabric made of cotton. Printed muslin is also available—for instance white muslin with a white printed pattern such as a fleur de lis looks particularly striking. Plain muslin is translucent and the printed pattern is opaque so the pattern shows up when the sun is shining. Other popular materials include voile which often contains silk—making it a slightly pricier option—yet one that can add a natural softness to any room.

Layering and combining different shades (printed and plain) can result in some of the most magnificent and dramatic effects being created. Experiment with having sheer drapes in two or more different colors, say plain white underneath and fuchsia pink sheer curtains over the top—the combination will shut out more light but still be translucent enough to give a glowing effect through the curtains. Sheer curtains can either be the sole window dressing or can be supplemented with heavier curtains or blinds - possibly in the event when the need for privacy overshadows the need for natural light.

Lace Curtains

Lace curtains are an attractive window covering which let the light into the room while shutting out unsightly views or the gaze of people passing by. Lace is an open-weave fabric which is made by looping, knotting or plaiting fine threads together to form intricate, delicate patterns. Sheer curtains made of lace have the ability to add a romantic, traditional feel to most rooms. A single lace panel can have a permanent position hung across a window and be coupled with heavier outer curtains which can drawn to provide additional cover at night-time.

Lace curtains can be backed with sheer, coloured linings to create interesting effects. Lace-making originated in north Italy in the sixteenth century—Venice, in particular, was a center for lace-making. Hand-made lace took a lot of work to produce and was worn as status symbol. Motifs or designs were created which could then be stitched on to netting or another patterned open-weave background. Techniques for making lace include crocheting, needlepoint or machine. Modern lace is made of linen, cotton, rayon, polyester or other man-made materials. There are different styles of lace available which reproduce traditional patterns:

— Batternberg lace is characterised by loops and curves with motifs of butterflies, hearts or flowers for a romantic, traditional look. This type of lace is a tape lace which is a narrow piece of lace produced by machine and then stitched onto the fabric.

— French lace is light and flowery in style. Lace-making in France originated in the sixteenth century influenced by Venetian designs but less severe and more fanciful.

— Making Irish crocheted lace became a popular means for the poor to extend their income when the potato crop failed. Young girls imitated needle-stitched Venetian lace to produce fine crocheted Irish lace which found its way into high society, including the court of Queen Victoria . Certain areas in Ireland became famous for their lace production.

— Victorian lace is perfect for period properties. It is possible to find antique lace curtains from the end of the nineteenth century when lace curtains were at the height of their popularity, but they are rare and not always in pristine condition. Alternatively there are modern curtains which are produced in a Victorian style to recreate the spirit of that era.

Net Curtains

Net curtains are made from fabric with an open weave pattern which is usually a netting pattern, as the name suggests. They are usually white or cream and usually used as an under curtain with heavier curtains that can be drawn over the top. They stay over the window all the time and are not raised, removed or drawn. Ready made net curtains are readily available over the Net or from department stores. White won't fade in the sunshine - and is probably the most popular choice.

Net curtains are the suburban choice for keeping nosy neighbours out while allowing the light in. Interior fashion has never moved away from the need for bright airy rooms and net curtains can help achieve this feel. Net window curtains can be made of voile, cotton, muslin or nylon. The cheapest ones are made of nylon. Muslin panels are an alternative to net window curtains. Muslin is a flimsy plain cotton fabric which makes an ideal window dressing. Nets can either have a plain net-like pattern or have motifs and more elaborate patterns interwoven—similar to those found in lace.

These need to be hand-washed - they are quite delicate so it is best not to put them in a machine. There are detergents designed for brightening net curtains on the market—this stops and repairs any discolouring. Net curtains can look quite drab after a while and they do collect dust so they should be washed regularly.

Beaded Curtains

Popularised in the trendy, colourful 1960s, beaded curtains have been decorating walls, windows and doorways for almost half a century. Traditionally used to separate rooms, camouflage closets, hide doors and increase privacy, beaded curtains have also made an appearance as part of the Asian 'feng-shui' decorating scheme. Beaded curtains made a comeback when the Asian decorating scheme of feng-shui soared in popularity. Designed to balance your life energy (or 'chi') by reorganising your living space, feng-shui uses these curtains as room dividers, designed to slow down the passage of your chi throughout your home.

Most curtains measure 36" by 72", which fits the dimensions for a standard doorway. If a doorway is larger that , it's easy to hang multiple curtains side by side. There are a number of different materials used to create beaded curtains:

— *Acrylic*: Acrylic beads are transparent bits of coloured plastic that have been molded into shapes ranging from simple balls and cubes to butterflies, skulls and celestial shapes. Acrylic beads are a good alternative to glass beads, which can chip and break if mishandled.

— *PVC*: Beaded curtains strung out of shaped pieces of PVC are typically composed of hollow circular and square shapes. Incorporating fewer strands than a typical beaded curtain, PVC curtains are better for decoration than for providing privacy or dividing a room.

— *Glass*: Beaded glass curtains are more expensive than curtains made from man-made materials. Emitting a pleasant tinkling noise, glass beads are best used away from high-traffic areas in the home as frequent handling may result in the beads cracking or breaking.

— *Bamboo*: Bamboo is a natural lightweight material popular for use in doorway curtains. Bamboo curtains make a soft swishing noise instead of the clackety-clack characteristic of glass or plastic beads. Easily dyed and coloured, bamboo can be manipulated to impart a design.

— *Wooden*: Wooden beads are a natural way to use a beaded curtain in your home. A bit sturdier than bamboo beads, wooden beads can be stained, painted or carved into any number of shapes. Some people prefer to leave the wood alone, allowing its natural grain to show.

— *Painted*: Beaded bamboo curtains can be made more decorative by painting or printing images onto them. Popular images include smiley faces, Navajo patterns, images of dolphins, yin yangs and peace signs, though famous paintings like DaVinci's Mona Lisa and Edvard Munch's The Scream have been reproduced.

Kid's Curtains

Kids curtains brighten up any child's room, adding fun flair to any decorating scheme. Long gone are the days of boring old fabric; today kids curtains come in a wide assortment of colors, themes and zany patterns. Try to stick to shorter curtains such as valances and café curtains rather than floor-length drapes when outfitting your child's bedroom or playroom; this makes it easier to vacuum the floor without having to worry about sucking up the curtains.

Keeping the curtains short prevents younger children from reaching, hanging on, or tearing down the material. It is also less likely that your child will trip over a short curtain when running around. Relatively inexpensive and machine washable, cotton is the preferred fabric when choosing kids curtains. Smudgy fingers and crumbs often gravitate to everything in a young child's path, so try to refrain from hanging flimsy, expensive fabrics in your child's windows.

When choosing curtains, keep in mind that kids grow quickly, resulting in constantly changing likes and dislikes. What your child prefers at age seven will probably be completely different from what he or she wants a year later. A good tip to keep in mind when choosing and budgeting for any child's décor is to avoid trends, which can rapidly lose favour. Try to choose a style that is sure to stick around for some time; for example, decorating with trendy cartoon characters or the latest hot pop group can backfire if they lose popularity.

Kids curtains come in such a wide variety of styles that it is nearly impossible not to find something to suit both parent and child. Try curtains printed with ballerinas for your little dancer, classic cartoon characters for your budding film critic and sports teams for the future athlete. Younger children might benefit from an alphabet or circus theme, which allow for any colour choice. Of course, any set of kids curtains are livened up with fun accessories; use baseball bats instead of curtain rods for a sports-theme room or hang a pair of ballet slippers or a cowboy hat on the end of the curtain rod.

Uses of Curtain Valances

Curtain valances cover the top of the curtains and hide unsightly tracks or fixtures. Curtain pelmets are a stiff, fixed cover which runs out from the wall and across the top of the curtains while valances are single short panels which attach to the curtain pole or track in the same way as the main drapes. They go across the top of the window for decoration and consist of one single piece of material or panel which stays in place whether the main curtains are open or closed.

Usually curtains and valances are bought together as a matching set but it can be worth experimenting contrasting materials, colors and styles to create a unique look. There are different styles of curtain valances. Panel valances are plain, short panels which attach to the curtain pole. Panels can be gathered or shirred for decoration. Shirred panels are where the material is gathered in parallel rows. The bottom hem doesn't have to be straight; it can either be longer in the middle or shorter to make the bottom curved. One alternative to curtain valances or pelmets is swag. This is where a panel is draped across the curtain rod so it dips in the middle and the ends are pleated or gathered so they fall in folds down the sides.

Box valances go around the top area of the window - ie comes out from the wall, across the top of the window and back towards the wall the other side to create a box shape. There is a type of curtain track with a clip on valance track which comes out in front of the main track. The valance attaches to the valance track and hides the track holding the curtain on the wall. Another method of attaching valances is to use medallion holdbacks or tiebacks which screw onto the wall and two curtain rods can be fitted to them, one for the valance and one for the main curtain.

Curtain Tiebacks

Using tiebacks correctly: Curtain tiebacks are used for holding drapes back from the window to allow more light in and to stop the curtains blowing around on a windy day. In addition to tucking the curtains out of the way when they are open, tiebacks are also an attractive window finishing. Tiebacks made out of the same fabric as the curtains are usually bought with the curtains as part of a matching set.

Tassel curtain tiebacks are made of threads braided into a rope with tassels on the end. They are usually available in a range of colors so that you can either match your curtains or pick a contrasting colour. Traditionally tiebacks are positioned two thirds of the way down the curtain so the hooks to hold the tieback in place are screwed about half way down the length of the wall. However you can have a curtain tieback around the center of the curtain or attached to the curtain rod, pulling the curtain back from about a third of the way down. You would need to use longer tiebacks to achieve this effect. Ornamental wooden or metal tiebacks screw into the wall next to the window and the curtain can be tucked behind. Metal curtain tiebacks are available in different finishes such as brass, bronze or iron and finials are attached to the end for decoration. Wrought iron tiebacks have striking designs and are sculptured into detailed patterns.

If the curtains are plain, you can get away with ornate, unusual tiebacks which are a feature in their own right. Finials can be attached the ends of plain metal tiebacks for decoration. These can be bought to match the finials on the end of the curtain pole. Antique tiebacks from the Victorian age were designed like a door knob with a metal plate that screwed into the wall or window frame and a long pin with a flower (or other design) for the head made of glass or wood. These can still be found - unfortunately the condition they are in can always be a bit of a gamble, with many of them being damaged.

Curtain Rods

Curtains are supported using either curtain rods or track depending on what sort of fitting the window or door lends itself to. Rods, or curtain poles, are the more attractive form of curtain support and can add to the decor. Track is the cheaper option but looks unsightly and should be covered if possible. If there is not enough space above the window for a curtain rod, then track has to be used instead. There are many different styles of curtain rod on the market, so finding a style in keeping with your home should not be a problem.

Plain wooden or metal poles can be dressed up with exotic finials and vice versa. Impressive wrought-iron poles with old-fashioned designs, such as a fleur de lis, look almost medieval. Metal curtain rods with a shiny brass finish look very smart. Consider the rest of the room and the curtains when choosing a curtain pole.

Rings and Finials: The poles should come with matching rings which slide onto the pole and have smaller metal rings hanging from them. The curtains have hooks threaded through the back of the curtain and can be attached to the curtain rings using these. Both the poles and the rings are visible. The poles can be finished off with curtain finials which slide on the end of the poles to stop the end rings falling off and for decoration.

Finials can be mixed and matched so you can have a plain pole with an ornate finial or an intricately-designed pole with a plain finial. Often curtain rods and finials are bought as a matching set. While curtain rods are usually bought with matching curtain rings, it can be fun experimenting with contrasting rings. Remember that the rings should be at least half an inch larger in diameter than the pole. Another option is to have the curtain stitched so the top hem forms a pocket big enough for the rod to fit through.

Tab top curtains have wide straps sewn across the top of the curtains which attach the curtain to the pole. Curtain rings are most the most common method and have the advantage that curtains can easily be taken down and put up without moving the curtain rod.

Fitting curtain rods to bay windows: Bay windows consist of three windows to fit in the three-sided bay; usually bay windows use flexible track which bends around the bay for curtains. However for older bay windows with thicker gaps between the panes, you can use curtain rods and still not lose too much light when the curtains are pulled back. You need one rod per window and the middle curtain will pull across to one side. Using tiebacks can help hold the curtain out of the pane. If there is not much room between the top of the window and the ceiling then using curtain poles may not be possible.

Double curtain rods: These have two parallel rods projecting from one set of brackets to allow for a curtain valance or having two layers of drapes. People may wish to have two layers of curtains if they want to have a thinner under layer which can be drawn to allow the light in but cover an unsightly view or stop people looking in.

The outer curtains would be heavier curtains which could be drawn at night-time. The other alternative is to have two sets of sheer drapes to create unusual effects with light and colour.

Curtain poles installation

Curtain poles are an attractive alternative to using track to support your curtains and are usually exposed, meaning that there is often call for some decorative flair to blend them into the feel of the room. They come in all sorts of styles and materials from plain simple poles to unusual, intricately-designed poles. They can only be fitted if there is enough space above the window—hence track is usually used for bay windows.

Curtain poles are attached to the wall, window frame or ceiling with brackets. Where the poles are fitted depends on how strong the supporting wall is. If the wall is soft and uneven it may be better to attach the curtain pole to the window frame which is likely to hold better. Another alternative would be to attach the pole to the ceiling. Remember it is not only the weight of the curtain pole that is an issue; the weight of the curtains needs to be taken into consideration as well.

The pole should be positioned about 4-6 inches above the window frame and if there is space either side of the window, then the pole should extend beyond the edge of the window frame to allow the curtains to be pulled back away from the window. Mark where the brackets should go in a soft pencil and then install the brackets according to the manufacturer's instructions. This usually involves drilling holes for screws. Fix one of the brackets and, attach the curtain pole and then fix the other bracket. Put one curtain ring on each end of the pole outside the bracket before attaching the curtain finials. This is to prevent any chance of the outside edge of the curtain being pulled across the window area.

Tension curtain rods use a spring to hold the rod in place i.e. there is no need for brackets, drilling or screws. These rods are more practical and would work best with a window treatment that hides the rod—for instance panel drapes with a pocket hem that the rod slides into. Double curtain poles for hanging two layers of drapes consist of two poles attached to a single bracket and should be installed in the same way as single curtain rods.

Working with brackets: Curtain rod brackets are used for fixing the rods or poles which will be used to support the curtains to the wall. Usually brackets are bought with the curtain pole to ensure they fit the pole correctly and match the rod's colour or style. However it is possible to purchase brackets, finials and curtain rings separately—and work towards creating a more personal look. Curtain rod brackets are fitted into the wall, window frame or ceiling depending on what is going to give the best support. Wall fittings are the most common but if the wall is too soft to support the weight of the pole and the curtains, then consider screwing the brackets into the window frame or the ceiling.

For recess windows you can get brackets that slot over the end of the pole in matching colors and styles so they are less noticeable. Alternatively use wooden brackets with a U shape for the rod to slot into and paint the wood the same shade as the wall so it blends in. When installing the brackets, it is important to follow the manufacturers' instructions as different designs require different set of procedures. Wooden brackets usually have a metal plate that is screwed on to the wall and then the bracket screws on to the plate. When deciding where to place the brackets, use a steel tape measure to measure the correct distance and use a soft pencil to mark where the holes should be drilled.

Space should be allowed either side of the window so the curtains can be pulled back away from the window frame. Leave about 4" above the window frame.

Discount Curtains

Many people are surprised to find that one of the most expensive accessories when decorating a window is the curtain itself. It's true; even a little bit of fabric can be expensive once it's tailored, hemmed and packaged for sale as a curtain. But with a little knowledge and a set of discount curtains, anyone can outfit a house without going broke.

Curtains vary so dramatically in price, style and quality that anyone can find what they want while still remaining cost conscious. Remember that the more area you need the more money you should plan to spend. For example, long panels and drapes can be more expensive than short shades and valances.

How much cash is required also depends on the type of fabric you plan to hang in your window. Velvets, wools, brocades and other lush fabrics can be very pricy. On the other hand, silk, crepes and sheers can also require quite a bit of money. Your best bet when searching for low prices is to turn to simple fabrics such as cotton, polyester and percale blends. Keep in mind, however, that these fabrics are more prone to fading when exposed to sunlight. Cost also increases when embellishments, embroidery and other decorative aspects are added.

If you know how to work a sewing machine, or simply consider yourself crafty, sometimes the best discount curtains are the ones you make yourself. Buying raw fabric is cheaper than buying finished curtains; all it takes is some concentration and a sewing needle to cut and hem them to size. Visit your local fabric and craft store to browse through their pattern books; you might find something you like. Sometimes the best deals can be found by buying your fabric in bulk. This can be great if you have numerous or extremely large windows. Purchase your fabric wholesale or visit a factory outlet store. Or go the simple route and hang a patterned or brightly coloured sheet in a window; no hemming required.

Curtain Patterns

— From chintz to check, trying to decipher (let alone choose) among the multitudes of curtain patterns is enough to drive almost anyone mad. Here are a handful of the most popular prints used in curtains patterns:

— Brocade is a popular pattern typically used in formal settings. Woven on a jacquard loom, brocade is characterised by a raised design, usually floral, on a flat surface of cotton, silk or wool. Available in medium to thick weights, brocade comes in any colour.

— Calico generally describes any type of cotton fabric printed with a simple, small repeating floral pattern. Calico is generally considered to be an inexpensive fabric pattern.

— Chintz describes a cotton fabric that features various multicoloured patterns (floral is quite common) on a lighter coloured background. Chintz is glazed for its characteristic smooth shiny finish.

— Damask is one of the most prevalent curtain patterns; similar to brocade, damask also incorporates a raised pattern and flat background though is somewhat thinner and more pliable than heavy brocade.

— Dotted Swiss involves a repeating polka dot pattern of three dimensional dots; this effect is accomplished by embroidering or weaving on the pattern. Sometimes the dots are simply pasted to the surface.

— Embroidery is where a needle threaded with thick embroidery thread (also called floss) is passed repeatedly through a slightly stiffer fabric to achieve a desired design. Typically created by hand, less expensive versions are machine made.

— Fleur de lis is one of the most traditional curtain patterns available. This familiar pattern repeats the stylised 'fleur de lis' or three petal flower over and over again on any type of fabric. This design is frequently executed in a damask or brocade style of weaving and is usually done in light coloured thread on a darker coloured background.

— Gingham is a plain, light coloured cotton or synthetic fabric checked with a darker second colour. Gingham is commonly seen in country inspired décor, making it a popular material for kitchens.

— India Print describes a curtain pattern where inked blocks are hand pressed onto cotton fabric to impart a desired design.

— Matelasse is similar to brocade and damask; however, unlike these two curtain patterns, matelasse is woven with two sets of warp, leaving the raised design slightly puckered and unfinished looking.

— Natural weaves mimic the fibres of hemp, burlap and jute. Natural weave cotton is purposefully left rough or unfinished, resulting in a fabric similar to canvas.

— Paisley describes a multicoloured pattern of swirling, repeating shapes. Paisley can be printed on any fabric though it is most common on thin cotton and synthetic weaves.

— Plaid involves a number of different colors combined in a grid-like pattern. Plaid often appears on thicker fabrics such as cotton or wool.

— Tapestry described a richly textured curtain pattern where each stitch appears to have been individually made. Tapestries used to be sewn by hand although today much less expensive versions are typically machine-made.

— Ticking is a vertically striped fabric incorporating a pattern of darker stripes on a light background. Ticking is named after the printed fabric traditionally used to cover mattresses.

Selecting Curtains

Selecting curtains for your home as part of a redecoration project, or for your brand new home can be a fun and exciting way to change the look of a room. However, there are many things to consider when you are choosing any type of window treatment including colour, style, the sun exposure and the type of room. No matter where you live you will want to consider the amount of sun exposure the room will be getting. If the windows are on the east or west side of the home they will be getting the most direct sunlight over the course of the year. If you live in a hot area you should choose window coverings and curtains that minimise the amount of heat that comes into the room. This will not only make you more comfortable, but will also cut down on your air conditioning bills.

In bedrooms, you may want to consider curtains or window coverings that severely limit the amount of morning sun that enters the room. This is good for people who don't want to wake up at the crack of dawn, or who don't want their children to wake up at the crack of dawn. You can find rolling screens or heavy shades that keep most light out. But, since the bedroom is a reflection of the person or people who sleep there, you might want to hang a decorative curtain or sheer over the screen to put an added touch of style and colour. You can also use a valance, swag, or cornice above the window.

For the kitchen, some people choose to leave these windows without a shade, and only use some kind of other curtain. Since privacy is not an issue typically in the kitchen, alight curtain is ideal for the kitchen, being used more for a decoration than anything else. For a family room or great room that has a sliding glass door, some people choose to use a heavier curtain that hangs on a rod or vertical shades as opposed to any other kind of curtain. Again, for decor purposes, it is very possible and quite nice to accent the door using some kind of additional curtain, for example a fabric that complements the fabric on the furniture.

In the bathroom, depending on the size of the window and whether or not there's a privacy issue, some people choose either cover the window with a light curtain on a rod, cover the window with a vinyl shade or something similar, or even not cover the window at all. New curtains are a fairly easy way to spruce up the look of any room in your home. Whether you purchase them or make them yourself, find a design and a colour that suits you and the others in your home. Remember to take all of the factors like sunlight exposure and privacy into consideration. Use your talents and imagination.

The next step on the road to choosing window dressings is to measure your windows and remember to take notes along with you when you go shopping! As well as ensuring that you have the correct drop, by measuring from the pole or track, to the required length, it is also important to choose the right width. As a general rule pencil pleated curtains should be 1.5 times as wide as the windows. Tab-top curtains on the other hand just need to lay flat when pulled across the window. When it comes to blinds you will need to decide whether you want your blinds to fit into the window recess or stand proud, before making a purchase. It is also worth remembering that many blinds can be trimmed to fit your exact window size.

Ready made curtains: These come in a variety of different styles to suit all price ranges. Lightweight voile panels are available, either patterned or plain in a choice of easy care polycotton or fine cotton. Sold singly, these great value curtains are suitable for use with rod or track and can also look terrific when hung from trendy curtain clips. If you prefer a smart, tailored look, check out the ready-made pencil pleat curtains, which come either lined or unlined. Alternatively, for something a little less formal choose fashionable tab top curtains that can be hung from a pole in seconds.

There is a vast selection of fabrics to choose from when it comes to selecting curtains. Smart cotton sateens, thick textural chenilles, classic checks, plain cottons and understated self-patterned fabrics are just some of the styles available. Most ready-made curtains are available in a range of standard sizes, the maximum drop being around 230cm. Matching tie-backs are also available in many ranges to help you achieve a totally co-ordinated look.

Blinds: Just as with curtains, blinds vary enormously in price and style. Inexpensive paper or bamboo roll-up blinds are great if you are just setting up home, as they'll look good without costing the earth. Smart PVC venetian blinds, available in a wide range of colours, are also good value for money. For a relaxed, contemporary look, Roman blinds in simple cotton and canvas are hard to beat. Special dim-out blinds, designed to cut out the light, are ideal for kids rooms. For humid environments like kitchens and bathrooms roller blinds made from manmade fabrics which help reduce mould growth make a practical choice.

Steps for Clean Curtains

Curtains should be cleaned often as they tend to

accumulate dust and dirt. And with a variety of cleaning options available, there's no excuse for neglecting them.

— Take down your curtains and inspect the back side of the fabric for signs of sun-rotting by stretching and feeling. If the curtains are sun-rotted, don't bother cleaning them. Shop for new curtains instead.

— Wash unlined curtains according to the instructions provided on the label.

— Have lined curtains professionally dry-cleaned to prevent possibly ruining them.

— Wash large curtains in your bathtub to prevent possible damage to your washing machine.

— Boil rusty curtain rings in vinegar to rediscover their shine. Rub soap on old curtain rods to make them run smoothly again.

— Toss your curtains into a dryer for a quick job. Add fabric softener to an air-dry setting and you've got fresh-smelling curtains in half an hour.

Dust your curtains frequently using a vacuum attachment. This way, you'll keep them clean without having to periodically take them down and put them back up. To keep a curtain from being sucked into the nozzle of the vacuum cleaner, use the lowest setting and place a stiff piece of plastic screening between the nozzle and the curtain.

11

MAINTENANCE OF BEDDING

Bedding is a generic term that refers to all types of material which make up a bed.

TYPES OF BED MATERIALS

Bed Sheet

A bed sheet (also known as a "flat bed sheet" or a counterpane) is a type of bedding—a large rectangular piece of cotton or linen cloth bed cover. It is this sheet that one typically lies on. They were traditionally white, but now often various patterns are used. They are larger than the bed, so they can be tucked under the mattress in order to be kept in place.

A "fitted" bed sheet is not a simple flat cloth, but is sewn to match the shape of the mattress. The corners are fitted with elastic so they can be stretched over the mattress, and then the edges can be tucked under the mattress. Sometimes confused with a comforter, it is usually found under a comforter, but over the mattress cover.

In many areas of the world a second flat bed sheet is lain on top of the sheet covering the mattress. One sleeps between the two bed sheets. Comforters and other bed covers are then placed on top of the second bed sheet.

In fiction, bed sheets are often knotted by prisoners in order to be used as a rope and escape by climbing down the window.

Blanket

A blanket is a type of bedding—a usually square—or rectangular-shaped piece of cloth generally intended to keep people warm, especially while they sleep. It can be distinguished from sheets by its thickness and its intention; the thickest sheet is still thinner than the lightest blanket, because blankets intend to warm people, while sheets are for hygiene, comfort and aesthetics.

Blankets are subdivided into many types, including quilts, duvets, and comforters depending on their thickness, construction and/or fill material. Blankets are typically made of wool, while sheets are made of cotton—wool tickles, cotton does not. Sometimes people will sleep with the blanket over their head. This can cause suffocation without proper ventilation.

Comforter

A comforter is a type of bedding—a soft flat bag used on a bed as a type of bed cover. It is filled with either an artificial material (such as polyester batting) or a natural material. A comforter usually doesn't cover the pillows or box spring of the bed. Its purpose is primarily decorative, since comforters don't provide much warmth, unlike blankets whose purpose is to provide warmth. A similar type covering made from feathers (often including down) is generally referred to as a duvet.

Duvet

A duvet is a type of bedding—a soft flat bag traditionally

filled with down or feathers, or a combination of both and used on a bed as a blanket. Duvets originally came out of rural Europe and were made of Eider, a type of duck's down, which is well known for its usefulness as an insulator.

Eiderdown is therefore used as a synonym of duvet, as is continental quilt. Duvets are still commonly used in Europe (especially in northern Europe and Scandinavia where it is the most common form of bed covering), and have become popular throughout the world in the late twentieth century.

Duvets reduce the complexity of making a bed, as it is a single cover instead of the combination of two sheets, blankets, and quilts or other bed covers, which is traditional in many parts of the world. Beds equipped with duvets are usually covered first with a flat or fitted bed sheet and then afterwards with a covered duvet. The cover is called a "duvet cover".

Nowadays, a duvet is sometimes filled with wool or artificial fibers (such as polyester batting or other artificial material). It is also sometimes referred to as a comforter, although comforters are primarily decorative while duvets are used for their warmth.

In eastern Australia it is called a "Doona", from a trademarked brand name derived from the Old Norse dunn meaning "down feathers". Though still registered to the Tontine company, the name "Doona" has become a generic term for a duvet or down quilt. A "sick day" from work is sometimes referred to as a "doona day". Originally the term continental quilt was the standard name used across Australia; some regions of Australia still use this term today.

For fit a Duvet Cover: Many people will struggle for literally minutes to fit duvet covers. This entry aims to crack the problem. The duvet should be laid flat out across the bed, with the dirty cover removed. The clean cover must be inside out. Put your hands inside the duvet cover and grasp the two corners furthest from the opening. Wearing it like a huge glove, carefully take hold of the top corners of the duvet.

Lift both the cover and the duvet and give the whole lot a little shake. The cover should fall down over the duvet, although you might need to move it along to get the opening over the top. Hold both in the air and continue shaking. You can either stand on the bed, letting gravity do all the work, or put the whole thing down and pick it up by gripping the sides nearer the bottom. Carry on shaking until the cover is at the bottom, then turn it upside down and repeat the glove trick on the bottom corners1 with another shake to settle it in smoothly.

Duvet Covers Guide

When researching and choosing your bedding, it is important to understand all the elements that make up comforter sets. This simple to follow duvet guide will explain all there is to know about choosing the right duvet covers and everything relating to duvets.

Thread Count

The thread count in a duvet refers to how closely knit the comforter threads are. In general, thread counts usually range between T150 and T220. With T180 and up being considered good quality duvet covers.

Design

There are different types of designs to consider when selecting duvets, both affecting the quality and in turn cost of the comforters set. Jacquard—is a 'woven' design, which tends to be more costly, as the design is more elaborate and therefore more labour intensive. The pattern of the duvet cover is woven into the fabric giving the look of the duvet cover longevity

Print—as the name says, will be a print of a particular design or pattern. It is 'printed' on to the duvet cover. A Print can be transferred to fabric by various methods. One way to transfer is a wet print, which is a direct colour to fabric transfer. Another way is the heat transfer, where the design is transferred from paper to fabric. This method contains a polyester fiber. Some prints can also be given a 'woven' affect, but the process of the weave is not done but rather a visual effect of the print.

Duvet Size Guide

You will find measurements of various duvets including, King Size Duvet, Queen Size Duvet and Twin Size Duvet.

Trims

Trims basically accentuate your bedding, it is the 'finishing' onto the edges. Typically, you will find bedding that are Knife Edged, Piped or Corded. Corded Edges are normally the most expensive because of the labor process. It looks like a cord is sewn onto the edges of the bedding or can also be used as an accessory on a pillow sham for example.

Stuffing

You must also be aware that the contents inside of the comforter will vary as well. If you would like a very thick and warm comforter, then search for one that is filled with 8-10 ounces. This weight is considered, 'Overstuffed'. If the comforter is filled with only 5-6 ounces then it will still keep you warm, but will not be as thick and will be of a lesser quality.

There are also different stuffing types in comforters. You must take note of this as some comforters will 'bunch up' or clump in certain areas over time, so in order to prevent this, look for one that is Bonded. This stuffing is sprayed with a special solution that will keep it from not shifting over time and will remain even for a longer period. Garnetted is the regular stuffing used.

Synthetic Duvets

Duvets which use synthetic materials rather than feathers are available for those with allergic tendencies. Whether it is due to the material used or the type of basting stitch used to keep the material in place, synthetic duvets seem somewhat less prone to creep and clump in the wee hours of the night. However, perhaps because synthetic duvets tend to be less heavy, they often have a difficult time staying properly attached to the cloth duvet covers.

Prior to the advent of synthetic duvets, duvet use was generally frowned upon for those with asthma, who are often prone to allergies. Furthermore, duvets can be a hiding place for dust mites, which are also known to aggravate asthma. Those with asthma are recommended to wash all bedding in hot water weekly, and this is especially true for duvet covers. Probably not worth mentioning but be sure to know your:

- Bed size
- Linen requirements
- Budget range for your comforter set

There are several great places on the Internet to buy duvet covers, if you found this information useful we urge you to check out some of our featured stores. Through their help, we are able to bring you this informational guide free of charge. Or course the stores featured are reliable, secure, and have a large selection of duvet covers to choose from.

Pillow

A pillow is a type of bedding—a small (and usually soft) support for the head, usually used while sleeping in a bed, or for the body as used on a couch or chair. There are also throw pillows which are pillows that are purely decorative and not designed for support or comfort. A husband pillow (also known as a bedrest) is a large, high-backed pillow with two "arms". It is conventionally used to prop oneself upright while in bed, as for reading or watching television. By analogy, in engineering and construction, supporting elements may also be called pillows.

Pillows are often used in the bed. The pillow has parts and can be dissected. Starting at the center, pillows contain a filler made from any of a variety of materials including, foam, synthetic fills, feathers, or down. Traditionally straw was a common filler, but this is uncomfortable and rarely used today. Historically feathers and down were the choice of the rich; today artificial fills are the most common.

The fill is then surrounded with a cover or shell made of some form of cloth or silk, commonly refered to as the pillow case. Pillows on furniture normally include a zipper in this cover so that the fill can occasionally be removed and the covering laundered. Bed pillows do not have this feature, and instead a case is used that can be frequently and easily removed and washed.

Even with regular washing, pillows tend to accumulate large amounts of dust and vast numbers of microbes among the fill and it is recommended that they be replaced every few years, especially for those with allergies. A rough rule of thumb: if you fold your pillow in half and it doesn't spring back, it's time to get a new pillow. Each corner of a pillow is refered to as a nib. When a pillow is placed on a flat surface the poof point is the crest of the pillow roundness.

Pillows have a long history, having been used by almost all settled peoples to enhance quality of life. They were originally used mainly by the wealthy, and have been found in Ancient Egyptian tombs. The difficulty of sophisticated dyes and sewing techniques lead to the development of pillows as an art form, with highly decorated pillows becoming prized commodities first in China and later in Medieval Europe. The Industrial Revolution saw the mass production of decorated textiles and decorated pillows became a common feature in millions of homes.

Cushion

A cushion (from Old French coisson, coussin; from Latin culcita, a quilt), is a soft bag of some ornamental material, stuffed with wool, hair, feathers, or even paper torn into fragments. It may be used for sitting or kneeling upon, or to soften the hardness or angularity of a chair or couch. Cushions and rugs can used temporarly outside, to soften a hard ground. They can be placed on sunloungers and used to prevent annoyances from moist grass and biting insects.

The cushion is a very ancient article of furniture; the inventories of the contents of palaces and great houses in the early Middle Ages constantly made mention of them. Cushions were then often of great size, covered with leather, and firm enough to serve as a seat, but the steady tendency of all furniture has been to grow smaller with time. Cushions were, indeed, used as seats at all events in France and Spain at a very much later period, and in Saint-Simon's time we find that in the Spanish court they were still regarded as a peculiarly honourable substitute for a chair.

In France, the right to kneel upon a cushion in church behind the king was jealously guarded and strictly regulated, as we learn again from Saint-Simon. This type of cushion was called a carreau, or square. When seats were rude and hard, cushions may have been a necessity; they are now one of the minor luxuries of life.

Makes a Lounge or Rug Softer

The term cushion is given in architecture to the sides of the Ionic capital. It is also applied to an early and simple form of the Romanesque capitals of Germany and England, which consist of cubical masses, square at the top and rounded off at the four corners, so as to reduce the lower diameter to a circle of the same size as the shaft.

Mattress

A mattress is a piece of bedding typically consisting of multiple layers of foams and fibers, along with an innerspring unit used to provide support to one's back during sleep. Mattresses are usually used along with a foundation, which might include metal springs or torsion bars on a wooden frame, which supports the mattress.

Increasingly, mattresses made with various foam materials such as latex foam, visco-elastic foam and other polyurethane type foam but without metal spring units are becoming common and accepted. Although mattresses are sold with fillings of air, water, or foam, innerspring or coil mattresses currently have over 80% of the market share in the U.S.

The fabric used to cover the exterior of a mattress is called mattress ticking. With modern production methods, it takes 10 to 60 minutes to make a mattress from start to finish. Most mattresses have a thickness from 6" to 14".

When does a mattress need replacing?

— After 7 to 15 years of use, although many people use their mattresses for many more years.

- Experts indicate that two adults sleeping nightly on a queen mattress will notice the padding, not the coils, breaking down after a period of 4 to 6 years. While the mattress will still be comfortable, it will no longer feel the way it did when first purchased.
- When laying a hand on the mattress with about 3 pounds-force and sliding it over the mattress lumps can be felt.
- When the user regularly wakes up feeling tired, stiff, achy and sore.
- When inner coils start springing out of the mattress.
- When the mattress shows very visible deformities.
- When the mattress looks old, frayed or worn.
- When the mattress is normally sagged, has lost its flat shape and there is an impression of the user sleeping on it, especially, a noticeable sag in the middle of it.
- When the box spring creaks and squeaks.
- When the user has difficulty finding a comfortable position to sleep in.
- A thing to consider is that a regular person exudes about 0.5 liters of liquid a night, although probably the majority of it evaporates. Mattresses normally absorb moisture from the body, so after years of use it is probably saturated with the salts of the perspiration.

Innerspring Mattress

A common innerspring mattress consists of 3 components:

- The spring mattress core, also called innerspring unit.
- The foundation, which many people call box spring (but it is not always a box spring)
- Upholstery layers, which encase the mattress core.

Spring Mattress Core

The core of the mattress is the most important part in the support of the body. In most modern mattresses (except for the foam-only ones), it is made up of steel coils springs, also known simply as coils. The spring mattress core is also called innerspring. It provides support to the set. Proper support is where the wire coils push back in response to weight deflection to hold the body in alignment.

The steel coil spring was invented during the industrial revolution and was first patented for use in a chair seat in 1857. Then, in 1871, Heinrich Westphal invented the innerspring mattress. He lived in Germany and died in poverty, having never profited from his invention.

Number of Coils

Basically, the more coils a mattress has, the more support it will give the user. As a general rule, very firm mattresses have a high coil count. Generally, but depending on the mattress size, they come with 300 to 800 coils. Depending on the size, 500 to 800 coils is considered firm. However, some expensive and comfortable mattress only have around 400 coils. and it takes as few as 312 coils in a full mattress to provide decent support. Assuming that the overall coil count is decent, a heavy duty innerspring mattress may also increase the longevity of the mattress for large users.

Gauge of the Coils

Obviously, heavy gauge (thick) coils will offer a great deal of support while light gauge coils will give less support. A low coil count and heavy gauge wire can pass as a firm mattress in the store, but it is likely that this mattress will become lumpy quickly because it does not have enough coils. Many premium mattresses feature 14-gauge (1.63 mm) coils. Coils are measured in quarter increments. The lower the number, the thicker the spring. With coils of 14 to 15.5 gauge (1.63 to 1.37 mm), it is important that the total coil count be high to compensate for the fact that they give so easily under pressure. A 12.5 gauge (1.94 mm) innerspring, the thickest typically available, may feel rock hard in a double mattress even with a coil count of 400 or less.

Generally, the number and quality of these interconnecting wires is not published by the manufacturers. If there are too few of these interconnecting wires a mattress can lose its shape more quickly than one that has an adequate amount. Mattresses that sag quickly usually have few interconnecting wires. There are some manufacturers that make individually pocketed coils, which avoid movement on different sides of the bed because they are not interconnected. However, the special pockets provide the support required by the coil instead of the interconnection with other coils.

Types of Coils

Construction-wise, most manufacturers claim to have the best coil-to-gauge ratio. However, there are only a few innerspring manufacturers and 4 general types:

Bonnel Coils

These are the oldest ones and most commonly used. They were adapted from buggy seat springs of the 19th century. They are still prevalent in low priced mattresses. They have an hour-glass shape, and the ends of the wire are knotted or wrapped around the top and bottom circular portion of the coil(round-topped and self tied).

Marshal Coils

Also called pocketed coils, they are individually pocketed and less frequently used. Might not be properly tempered. The brand Simmons uses pocketed coils in their mattresses.

Offset Coils

Bonnell coils evolved into Offset coils, which are currently popular, but happen to be the most expensive ones. They are almost identical to the Bonnell coils, except that the top and bottom circular part of the coils have flat or straight sides, which allow for better hinging action when they are placed together in a spring unit, and which can be easily aligned. Brands as Stearns and Foster use regular Bonnell coils in their mattresses. An evolution of the offset coils brought the elimination of the knot that tied the end of the wire to the coil.

In other words, offset coils might be tied off or feature a loose end (sensory arm). These are called "open end offset coils". These improvement gave offset coils an extra turn of working wire for greater spring action on each end of the coil. However, loose ends increase the odds that a spring will begin to punch through the padding. Brands like Sealy and Spring Air use open end offset coils in their mattresses.

Continuous Coil

They look like double wire spirals or loose ringlets, creating a network of wire that runs nonstop through the entire bed. The brand Serta uses continuous coils in their mattresses.

Foundations

Although in the past the foundation actually contained

springs, increasingly today this foundation functions primarily to elevate the mattress, serving no ergonomic function. There are 3 main types of foundations:

Traditional Wood Foundation

It is usually made of of pine or similar hard wood. It usually has 7 or 8 support slats, covered with cardboard or biverboard. This type of foundation, called by the industry a zero deflection unit, increases the feeling of firmness or stability.

Box Spring

It features extra-heavy-duty springs. If the springs match the mattress it is called a coil upon coil box spring. Since a box spring has coils, it generally increases the give in the mattress, which in turn produces a softer or bouncier feel.

Grid Foundation

It is a combination of steel and wood.

Upholstery Layers

The mattress core is covered by several soft materials, which provide cushioning and comfort. Some manufacturers call the mattress core by the name "Support layer" and the cushioning materials by the name: "Comfort layer". The "Comfort layer"can be divided into three sub-layers: Insulator, Middle upholstery and Quilt. Aside from the number and gauge of the coils, the upholstery layers are used to differentiate the different "qualities" of mattresses that manufacturers produce.

Insulator: This layer separates the mattress core from the upholstery, and it is usually made of fiber or mesh, with the intention of keeping the middle upholstery in place.

Middle upholstery: The middle upholstery comprises all types of materials on top of the insulator and beneath the quilt. It is usually made from materials that give maximum comfort: Regular foam, visco-elastic foam, felt, polyester fibers, cotton fibers, egg-crate foam, non-woven fiber pads, etc.

Quilt: The quilt is a top layer of the mattress made of light foam or fibers stitched to the underside of the ticking, and provides the immediate soft texture that the user feels when lying on a mattress. The quilt can be firm or soft and plush. The protective fabric cover which encases the support and comfort layers of the mattress is called ticking. It is usually made to match the foundation and comes in a wide variety of colours and styles.

Most ticking is made of synthetic fibers like polyester, latex and acrylic, or of natural materials such as cotton, silk & wool. The ticking produces the look and feel of the mattress, so it is usually soft to the touch and attractive to the buyer (at least that is what manufacturers intend to create).

Choosing Mattress

There is no proven scientific way of finding the right mattress, so the best advice is to try it out.

Testing a mattress

— The prospective buyer should lie on it at for least 10 minutes, trying different positions.

— Lying on the back: If a user slides his/her hand under the small of the back, and it is very easy and his/her shoulders and hips are uncomfortable, the mattress is too hard. If there is no space between the user's back and the bed, it's too soft.

— Rolling over: If it takes a lot of effort, then the bed is too soft. If it uncomfortable for the user's hips and shoulders it is too hard.

— The user should test the mattress on the type of base that it will be used on.

— If the bed is for two people, both users should try it at the same time.

What to look for

— The mattress should be designed to conform to the spine's natural curves and to keep the spine in alignment when laying down.

— It should have perimeter edge support. Usually, this will be a heavy gauge border rod, however, in some high end models, a high density foam encased spring unit will provide firmer edge to edge comfort and support.

— It should be designed to distribute pressure evenly across the body to help circulation, decrease body movement and enhance sleep quality.

— It should be designed to minimise the transfer of movement from one sleeping partner to the other. The marshall coil and visco-elastic memory foam designs achieve this better than traditional coil systems.

— On a same size mattress, more coils of a lower gauge (thinner) may give better support and last longer than fewer coils with a higher gauge (thicker). A good warranty, 15 years being the best, will ensure your lower count-higher gauge coil mattress is of lasting quality.

FIRMER

There are 3 main sleep positions: Back, stomach and side.

During a night's sleep, most people use more than one position. The sleeping position determines which part of the body will interface with the mattress, which in turn determines the amount of stress to the body.

Firm Preference

— Orthopedic doctors usually recommend a firm mattress because it will not allow back or stomach sleepers to sag into the surface at unnatural angles. Air, water or foam mattresses are not generally recommended because they do not provide this level of support.

— Stomach sleepers probably need a firmer mattress to prevent spinal distortion that can result in back pain when waking up.

— It is easier to soften up a firm mattress with the proper padding or bedding, than it is to firm up an overly soft one that is causing a backache. A firm or very firm bed might be topped with a 3" visco-elastic foam pad giving the user the best of both worlds: Good support and soft cushioned feel.

Soft Preference

— Side sleepers usually face the greatest amount of weight on the smallest areas of the body thereby creating pressure points, which reduce circulation and can be a cause of the tossing and turning during sleep. A side sleeper will probably want a softer mattress, to minimise pressure points, especially if they have a very curved or rounded figure.

— A study of sleep quality and bed firmness showed that 4 of 9 male subjects slept significantly better on softer mattresses and 2 on the harder mattresses.

Not firm nor soft

— Back sleepers need a mattress that offers enough support to fill in the gaps in the contour of the back, while at the same time providing enough comfort, according to the user's preference.

Firm AND soft

— The brand Simmons currently produces King and Queen sized mattresses with a softer side and another firmer side, for the different tastes of the sleeping partners. Furthermore, there is a "Sleep number" bed that inflates and deflates inner air chambers to make it harder or softer, with separate controls and air chambers for both sides of the mattress, also to adjust to the different comfort preferences of the sleeping partners.

Fluff and Sag

Fabric is the most expensive element of mattress construction. Wool, silk, foam and cotton all increase the cost of the mattress. Thick layers of padding are more likely than the springs to compress to the point of feeling like the mattress is sagging. The fabric, foam or cotton eventually become concave because thick plush or pillowtop components eventually break down even if the springs do not. Unlike an eggcrate or other forms of padding, the mattress inner components cannot be removed and replaced when damaged.

Twin & Double are 75 inches long; Queen & King are 80 inches long; California Queen & California King are 84 inches long. According to experts, a mattress should be at least 6 inches longer than the tallest person who will be sleeping on it. Be aware that the bigger the mattress, the more expensive the sheets.

Maintenance and care

— A new mattress should be put on a firm base. Never on a saggy base.

— Most manufacturers of box spring mattresses suggest that the consumer should regularly rotate and flip the mattress and box spring.

— Otherwise, even the most expensive mattress will fail. Most manufacturers recommend to rotate the mattress (180 degrees, so the head of the bed becomes the foot) every 3 months and to turn the mattress at least twice a year. Some manufacturers recommend to alternately turn and flip the mattress once every two weeks for the first three months and then twice per year after that.

The foundation should also be turned every 12 months. All mattresses need to be rotated to reduce wear patterns that develop over time. It must be noted that since around 2000, several manufacturers started producing one-sided models that cannot be flipped and in some cases should not be turned either.

— Do not wet a mattress. An impermeable mattress protector can be used to keep it clean.

— Use a vacuum cleaner for regular cleaning. Vacuuming is the only recommended way to clean a mattress.

— Use a good quality washable mattress pad to keep the mattress free from stains. If stained, use mild soap with cold water and rub lightly. Do not soak a mattress or foundation.

— The mattress should not be lifted or carried using the handles, which are only for positioning it.

— The mattress should not be folded or bent.

— It is not good to habitually sit on the same spot of the mattress edge.

The tempurpedic mattress, or foam memory mattress, is the latest development in the science of sleep. They're made from Tempur material, foam made up of billions of spherical cells that are sensitive to temperature and weight. This means that where your body is making most contact with the surface of the mattress, the softer the mattress becomes. In cooler areas, where your body isn't making as much contact with the surface, the mattress remains firm. In this way, the tempurpedic mattress molds itself to your body.

The foam in tempurpedic mattresses is known as viscoelastic foam, whereas the foam usually used in mattresses is known as polyurethane foam. Viscoelastic foam doesn't have the springiness of regular polyurethane foam. This is where it gets a little confusing; we usually value springiness in a mattress because it's much better than sagginess. But springiness isn't always good. The springiness in conventional mattresses means that it "pushes back" when you lie on it, in proportion to the weight exerted on it.

This means that a conventional mattress pushes back at your body's lowest points; the base of the spine, the heels and the back of the head. Because of this pressure, these areas are where you're most likely to get pressure sores from a conventional mattress.

The viscoelastic foam in a tempurpedic mattress isn't springy at all because it is made of viscous. Viscous acts like a very thick fluid when it warms up in response to body contact. (Temperature-sensitivity is another way in which it differs from regular foam.) This means that it draws back from your pressure points rather than pushing back at them. It takes much longer than regular foam to react to pressure; this means that it gives way to your body slowly, and takes a corresponding amount of time to regain its original shape. This is why it's sometimes called memory foam.

The word "tempurpedic" is one of those brand names, like Hoover or Laz-e-Boy, which has become a generic term for the product. The original formula for memory foam was developed by NASA to help astronauts handle the effects of G-force. However, it was a Swedish foam company that first adapted the material for consumer use, creating the Tempur-Pedic Swedish Mattress. Because of this, tempurpedic mattresses are also known as "Swedish mattresses". Since then, other memory-foam mattresses have come on the market, and these are sometimes referred to as "tempurpedic" too; that doesn't mean they're made by the Tempur-Pedic company.

The main advantage of a memory foam mattress is the way it molds itself to your body. This combination of firmness and give is what makes for a good night's sleep and reduces the risk of developing bedsores. But there are other advantages too: weight on one part of the mattress doesn't affect other parts of the mattress. This is great for anyone who shares a bed with a restless partner, as their tossing and turning won't disturb you.

Some advertisements have shown people jumping up and down on one side of a tempurpedic mattress while a glass of wine balances on the other side. This isn't camera trickery—it's really possible. Another advantage of brand-name Tempur-Pedic mattresses is that they are designed to suit people with allergies, so dust mites shouldn't bother you.

The yielding nature of the viscoelastic foam means that it's hard to sit up and read in bed without slowly sinking into the mattress. You may also find that it's harder to move about in bed, as the memory foam creates a comfortable niche for your body. Some people find that they're stiff in the morning from having slept in the same position all night.

Brand-name: Tempur-Pedic mattresses cost about twice as much as good-quality regular mattresses: between $1000 and $2000 for a queen-sized mattress. However, memory foam mattresses from other manufacturers can be cheaper. For example, the Bergad Isoform mattress costs less than $1000. It is also possible to purchase a mattress "topper" which goes on top of your regular mattress and gives the effect of a memory foam mattress. These cost around $100, so they're a good budget alternative, although most users agree that they're not as good as the real thing.

The secret to buying discount mattresses is to avoid being blinded with science. Mattresses at the top end of the market are usually marketed as being the ultra-scientific answer to all your aches and pains. They have mysterious, but essential-sounding features such as "lumbar cradles" and "mega-edge support", and they all compete to have the largest coil count. It's easy to get carried away by the hype and start thinking that all these whistles and bells are essential to your health and happiness. That's the mindset that stops people taking advantage of good deals on discount mattresses; they worry that buying a no-frills mattress will lead to a poor night's sleep, or even back pain.

This belief is almost always false; if you have no existing back problems, it's unlikely that you need an expensive specialist mattress. As a general rule, if you don't understand the scientific principles behind a mattress's design—and the salesperson in the store can't explain in a way you understand—then it's probably not necessary that you pay extra for this special design.

The Internet is the best place to start shopping around for discount mattresses. You can easily compare the deals from different manufacturers without moving from your home. You should also visit your local furnishing stores and look out for sales. The sale price of a mattress in a store isn't always the lowest price you can get for it, so always check the Internet to see if it's possible to get a lower price, either directly from the manufacturer or from a discount site.

One good trick is to approach the manager of your local furnishing store and offer to buy the display mattress. They can't sell this at the regular price, as it is considered shop-soiled, so they may be willing to offer you a good price. The discount price you pay for a mattress depends on a variety of factors: the brand, the quality and your luck. Well-known brands of mattress normally cost between a few hundred dollars and a couple of thousand dollars.

If you shop around for bargains, you might be able to find such brand mattresses for less than half the price. Mattresses from less well-known retailers are cheaper, and you might be able to find one for less than $100. The discount price is usually in proportion to the recommended retail price for the mattress, so, for example, don't expect to buy a genuine foam memory mattress for less than $700.

Other tips for buying discount mattresses: Never buy a second-hand mattress. You don't get a manufacturer's guarantee, you can't be sure it's hygienic and many older mattresses aren't fire-retardant. They're not even much cheaper than discounted new mattresses.

Always check that the mattress is fire-retardant. State law varies about mattress fireproofing, so you will need to check for yourself. Don't pay extra for features such as attractive ticking—decorative details are a waste of money when you're going to throw a sheet over the mattress anyway. Always make sure there's a returns policy that allows you to get your money back if the mattress doesn't work for you. Returns policies usually let you bring the mattress back within either 30 or 60 days.

QUILT

A quilt is a type of bedding—a bed covering composed of a quilt top, a layer of batting, and a layer of fabric for backing, generally combined using the technique of quilting. Another technique for creating a quilt is tying. This method is easier and more forgiving if the quilt is made by hand. A tied quilt is called a hap. Many quilts are made with decorative designs; indeed, some quilts are not used as bed covering at all, but are rather made to be hung on a wall or otherwise displayed.

In British English, quilt is another way of saying duvet, and wadding is another way of saying batting. The quilt top is created either from blocks or one whole piece of cloth. In the more common case of blocks, a number of techniques are used to create the blocks. The blocks are then sewn together, either edge to edge, or with separator strips of cloth called sashing. Borders are then often added to help set off the piece, and then a binding is added to edge the quilt after the quilting is done.

As an example, the "science" quilt image above has 35 blocks arranged in a 5x7 pattern, set with a sashing of green strips combined with red squares at the corners of the blocks, and a white binding, but no border strips.

BIBLIOGRAPHY

Altpeter, Dorothy. *How to make braided rugs.* New York: Harper, 1949.

American Home Laundry Manufacturers' Association. *Proceedings of the 1st-national home laundry conference.* Chicago: The Association, 1900.

Balderston, Lydia Ray and Margaret C. Limerick. *Laundry manual.* Philadelphia: Avil printing company, 1902.

Benjamin, D. H. *The launderer. A practical treatise on the management and the operation of a steam laundry.* Cincinnati: The Starchroom publishing co., 1900.

Bradbury, F. *Carpet manufacture.* Belfast Ire; London etc; Boston Mass: The author; agents: J. Heywood; Lord and Nagle company, 1904.

Frederick, Christine. *"You and your laundry".* New York: Hurley Machine, 1922.

Friend, Mata Roman and Hazel Shultz. *Clothing.* New York: D. Appleton, 1933.

Harvey, Arthur. *Laundry chemistry, a manual on the chemistry of laundry materials and methods.* New York; London: Chemical Pub. Co.; Technical Press, 1936.

Hunter, George Leland. *Decorative textiles; an illustrated book on coverings for furniture, walls and* floors, *including damasks, brocades and velvets, tapestries, laces, embroideries, chintzes, cretonnes, drapery and furniture trimmings, wall papers, carpets and rugs, tooled and illumined leathers.* Philadelphia and London, Grand Rapids: J.B. Lippincott company; The Dean-Hicks company, 1918.

Imperial Chemical Industries ltd. *Laundry washing and bleaching.* Birmingham Eng: Printed at the Kynoch Press, 1935.

Jackman, Agnes Browne and B. Rogers. *The principles of domestic and institutional laundrywork.* London: E. Arnold & co., 1934.

Parker, R. G. and British Launderers' Research Association. *The control of laundry operations, being an introduction to the application of scientific principles to laundry processes.* Hendon: The British launderers' research association, 1925.

INDEX